Bloomsbury CPD Library: Raising Attainment in the Primary Classroom

Sonia Blandford and Catherine Knowles

BLOOMSBURY EDUCATION

LONDON OXFORD NEW YORK NEW DELHI SYDNEY

BLOOMSBURY EDUCATION
Bloomsbury Publishing Plc
50 Bedford Square, London, WC1B 3DP, UK

BLOOMSBURY, BLOOMSBURY EDUCATION and the Diana logo are trademarks of
Bloomsbury Publishing Plc

First published in Great Britain 2018

A catalogue record for this book is available from the British Library

ISBN: PB: 978-1-4729-5200-4; ePDF: 978-1-4729-5201-1; ePub: 978-1-4729-5199-1

2 4 6 8 10 9 7 5 3 1 (paperback)

Typeset by Integra Software Services Pvt. Ltd.
Printed and bound by CPI Group (UK) Ltd, Croydon, CR0 4YY

MIX
Paper from
responsible sources
FSC® C013604

All papers used by Bloomsbury Publishing Plc are natural, recyclable products
from wood grown in well-managed forests. The manufacturing processes
conform to the environmental regulations of the country of origin.

To find out more about our authors and books visit www.bloomsbury.com
and sign up for our newsletters.

Contents

Acknowledgements

We would like to thank all those who have contributed their thoughts and reflections on raising attainment. Our particular thanks to Achievement for All and the many schools that have engaged with us over the years; and our thanks to the headteachers and teachers who contributed their time in the development of the case studies. Thank you. And finally, with many thanks to the team at Bloomsbury for their support and guidance in writing this book.

How to use this book

The Bloomsbury CPD Library provides primary and secondary teachers with affordable, comprehensive and accessible 'do-it-yourself' continuing professional development. This book focuses on raising attainment in the primary classroom.

The book is split into two halves: Part 1 **Teach yourself** and Part 2 **Train others.**

Part 1: Teach yourself

This part of the book includes everything you need to improve your practice in raising attainment in the primary classroom. It is split into four stages.

Stage 1: Assess

As well as providing an introduction to the main areas of focus for raising attainment, Stage 1 includes a self-assessment questionnaire for you to start thinking about your practice and how you can improve on it. It will help you to start identifying your strengths and weaknesses and to start thinking about how you can take responsibility for your own professional development.

Stage 2: Improve

Stage 2 includes details of the key areas of focus for raising attainment and what you do in practice and how you can do it better. The idea of using evidence-based practice and doing your own research is considered, along with theorists who have influenced educational practice over the years.

Stage 3: Evaluate

Stage 3 allows you to reflect on what you have learnt from this book. It provides an opportunity for you to evaluate your practice and personal professional development. It encourages you to think about raising attainment in the context of the challenges you face, how you can overcome them and how your wellbeing and job satisfaction are enhanced by making a few changes to practice.

Stage 4: Excel

The final section of Part 1 looks ahead to the development of leadership skills and how these can enhance your practices as a leader of learning in the classroom and your own professional development.

This comprehensive self-teach guide also includes teaching tips, to do lists at the end of each chapter and recommendations for how you can share your ideas and practice with other teachers in your school and beyond. A further reading recommendation or title to discuss in a CPD reading group is also included as well as a useful blogpost to read in Bloggers' corner.

By the end of Part 1 you will have assessed, improved and consolidated your strategies for raising attainment in the primary classroom.

Part 2: Train others

Now that you are an expert in raising attainment in the primary classroom it's time to train others in your school! External training can be expensive and in-house training is hugely valuable as it can be made relevant to your training context – the teachers and children in your school. Whether it is a quick 15-minute training session, a series of twilight sessions, 30-minute sessions or an INSET day, there is advice and training plans in this part of the book to help you get started, plan and implement training on raising attainment in your classroom and across the school. This section includes:

- Advice on how to run effective professional development for raising attainment.
- Training plans for running quick 15-minute CPD sessions, a series of one-hour twilight sessions and a series of 30-minute sessions, which can all be run over a term/two terms, and details of how the plans can be used for INSET training days.
- Advice on how to evaluate the success of your CPD.

See page 152 for an overview of the training plans.

Online resources

For templates, questionnaires and PowerPoints from the book please visit: www.
bloomsbury.com/CPD-library-raising-attainment

Good luck with teaching yourself and training others! Keep us updated on your
progress by tweeting using #BloomsCPD.

Part 1

Teach yourself

1

What's it all about?

[A]n effective teacher increases access and raises aspirations as a means to improving achievement, an inspirational teacher improves achievement in a way that changes pupils' aspirations, and in so doing, improves their life chances by securing access to continued achievement and self-fulfilment. (Blandford and Knowles, 2013)

This book is about your role in the achievement of all children and pushing back against any practice that does not improve their life chances through education. Most teachers come into the profession wanting to make a difference in children's lives. Many would like to do it better; and this book, written to support teachers, leaders and wider professionals in the primary setting, shows you how to do that. Teaching is an increasingly challenging career. Commitment, collaboration and communication between teachers, leaders and the school community are essential elements for effective practice. The complexity of the educational landscape requires us to be supportive of each other with kindness and professionalism in equal measure. From the many teachers we have spoken to across the country, the message is the same; they *think*, after initial training, that they should know everything. A disturbing feature of our educational culture, it should not be like this. 'Initial teacher education' is self-defined and needs to be supported and further developed throughout your career. Continuing professional development is available in all major professions from law to medicine and should underpin the professional journey of all teachers.

Building the core

Good teachers never stop learning. They develop a framework for high-quality teaching and learning founded on aspiration, access, achievement and inclusion. Having put a firm base in place, knowing where the children are in their learning, where they are going and how to get them there, is more clear-cut. In essence, it is about leading learning in the classroom and building the core in children:

1. Aspiration: *I can*
2. Access: *I do*
3. Attainment: *I have*
4. Achievement: *I am*

It means:

- knowing the pupils and how they learn
- having high aspirations for their learning
- deconstructing barriers to learning
- giving children a sense of ownership of learning
- taking a more individualised approach to their learning

- keeping good records
- providing wider opportunities
- developing children's skills for future learning and careers
- decisively engaging parents and carers in the process
- monitoring and evaluating your own practice in these areas.

A strong framework for practice, engaged in every lesson, every day, provides a firm foundation for self-betterment. Gaps in knowledge, understanding and skills are more easily identified and it provides the *space* for rethinking practices and approaches. Through self-reflection, you will 'know' what you don't know and want to make it your business to find out. We'll look at this more in Chapter 2.

Rising to the challenge

Peter Jones of the *Dragon's Den*, in his analysis of successful entrepreneurship, highlights the benefits of learning from mistakes and always looking towards the future, a useful lesson for self-reflection:

> [T]here are no failures in this world, only events that give you feedback. (Jones, 2008)

All professional development has at its focus better outcomes for all children, no matter what their challenges, background or needs. We know that one in five children and young people does not achieve expected outcomes due to the disadvantages, challenges or needs they experience; and one in six children lives in poverty. Disadvantage in all its forms builds multiple and systemic barriers that prevent young people from achieving all they can. Too many children in this country are being left behind at a young age. It does not have to be like this; with the right approach in school and the support of their parents and carers, the multiple barriers that some children face are easily disassembled.

Classrooms need to be places of early action. Teachers help, when they support children in building their 'core strengths': *Aspiration – I can; Access – I do; Attainment – I have* and *Achievement – I am*. This defines the confidence and ability to learn and develop and the skills to participate in society. Children and young people experiencing disadvantage and underachievement often lack confidence, find learning challenging, may develop differently and can have limited participation in society. Underlying factors, or needs, may be cognitive, physical, emotional or social; each is manifest in a fundamental lack of progress of the child or young person when compared to their peers. This applies to both low- and high-ability children.

It is largely the teacher who creates the right environment for learning in the classroom. This is more effectively developed and sustained when the foundational blocks are in place: aspiration, access, achievement and inclusion. From this a framework for practice flows, enabling a better focus on children's learning and development.

Chapter 1 takeaway

Teaching tip

As a leader of learning in the classroom, you have the freedom to identify and make changes – in essence, to use new thinking on old questions. Here are a few questions to support you in making change:

- Consider the aspirations you have for the pupils in your class. Are they high enough for each child? How could you raise your aspirations for each child?
- Consider your pupils' aspirations. Do all pupils have high aspirations for their own learning and achievement? How could you raise their aspirations?
- Consider your classroom practice. Could you do more to enable every child to access teaching and learning? What could you do to remove those barriers (think of Pupil Premium pupils and those with SEND)?
- How do you currently engage parents and carers in their child's learning? How could you do this better?
- Consider relationships within your classroom. What could you do to improve pupil–pupil, pupil–teacher, teacher–teacher and parent–pupil–teacher relationships/interactions?

Pass it on

Commitment, collaboration and communication between teachers, leaders and the school community are essential elements for effective practice. Organise an informal CPD session for your colleagues, doing an audit of where and how you apply aspiration in your classroom. Consider what it means to you and how you are developing it in practice.

Share and tweet

Tweet, using the hashtag #BloomsCPD: raising attainment for all is about changing the way we think, act and engage.

CPD book club recommendation

Born to Fail? Social Mobility: A Working Class View by Sonia Blandford

(See bibliography)

This books provides a good insight into looking at the same questions with new thinking, prompting the reader to think about aspiration, access and achievement in a real context.

Bloggers' corner

The NfER (National Foundation for Educational Research) has topical and relevant blogs in their news section. Available at: www.nfer.ac.uk

TO DO LIST:

❑ Reflect on what aspiration, access and achievement mean, and what they mean in practice.
❑ Discuss with colleagues how you could further develop them.
❑ Consider the extent to which your classroom is inclusive. How could you make it more inclusive?
❑ Read *Born to Fail? Social Mobility: A Working Class View* by Sonia Blandford.
❑ Look up and read some of the NfER blogs on primary assessment.

2 Self-assessment

The best way to bring about change in the classroom is through self-reflection on your own practice; the starting point is a self-assessment of your current practices and approaches. Interaction with educational theory can transform our knowledge base, but it is through focused self-reflection that we find new ways of thinking and applying that in practice. Quality teaching and learning is characterised by inclusive practices, with a focus on improving outcomes for every child and young person. An audit of your current practice provides the baseline for change. This chapter will focus on how you self-assess your practices and approaches to raising attainment for every child and in so doing will enable you to identify your strengths, areas of challenge and areas for further development.

How to complete the self-assessment questionnaire

On the pages that follow, there is a self-assessment questionnaire to encourage you to start the 'teach yourself' process by thinking very carefully about your current approach to raising attainment before you jump into trying to improve it.

When you are reviewing your practice and trying to form a clear view of where you are now and what the next steps will be, there are many ways of approaching it – your approach will depend on you as a person. For some people, it is useful to go with your gut feeling and listen to the first thing that comes into your mind – your instinctual answer. For others, it is a better approach to spend a good amount of time really mulling over the self-assessment questions slowly and in detail.

Quick response approach

If your preference for the self-assessment is to go with your gut feeling only, then simply fill in the quick response section after each question with the first thing that comes into your mind when you ask yourself the question. Do not mull over the question too long; simply read carefully and answer quickly. This approach will give you an overview of your current understanding and practice regarding raising attainment for every child in the classroom and will take relatively little time. Just make sure you are uninterrupted, in a quiet place and able to complete the questionnaire in one sitting with no distractions so that you get focused and honest answers.

Considered response approach

If you choose to take a more reflective and detailed approach, then you can leave the quick response section blank and go straight on to reading the further guidance section under each question. This guidance provides prompt questions and ideas to get you thinking in detail about the question being asked and is designed to open up a wider scope in your answer. It will also enable you to look at your experience and pull examples into your answer to back up your statements. You may want to complete it a few questions at a time and take breaks, or you may be prepared to simply sit and work through the questions all in one sitting to ensure you remain focused. This approach does take longer, but it can lead to a more in-depth understanding of your current practice, and you will gain much more from the process than the quick response alone.

Combined approach

A thorough approach, and one we recommend, would be to use both approaches together regardless of personal preference. There is clear value in both approaches being used together. This would involve you firstly answering the self-assessment quick response questions by briefly noting down your instinctual answers for all questions. The next step would be to return to the start of the self-assessment, read the further guidance and then answer the questions once more, slowly and in detail, forming more of a narrative around each question and pulling in examples from your own experience. Following this you would need to read over both responses and form a comprehensive and honest summary in your mind of your answers and a final view of where you feel you stand right now in your approach to raising the attainment of every child.

This is the longest of the three approaches to this questionnaire but will give you a comprehensive and full understanding of your current practice, thoughts and feelings in relation to raising the attainment of every child. You will be surprised at the difference you see between the quick response and the considered response answers to the same questions. It can be very illuminating.

- I have done this self-assessment before.
- I only want a surface-level overview of my current understanding and practice.
- I work better when I work at speed.
- I don't have much time.

Quick

- I have never done this self-assessment before.
- I want a deeper understanding of my current understanding and practice.
- I work better when I take my time and really think things over.
- I have some time to do this self-assessment.

Considered

- I have never done this self-assessment before.
- I have done this self-assessment before.
- I want a comprehensive and full understanding of my current understanding and practice and want to compare that to what I thought before taking the self-assessment.
- I have a decent amount of time to dedicate to completing this self-assessment.

Combined

Fig. 1 How should I approach the self-assessment questionnaire?

Rate yourself

The final part of the self-assessment is to rate yourself. This section will ask you to rate your confidence and happiness in each area that has been covered in the questionnaire, with a view to working on these areas for improvement throughout the course of the book. The table on page 12 shows how the scale works: the higher the number you allocate yourself, the better you feel you are performing in that area.

Rating	Definition
1	Not at all. I don't. None at all. Not happy. Not confident at all.
2	Rarely. Barely. Very little. Very unconfident.
3	Not often at all. Not much. Quite unconfident.
4	Not particularly. Not really. Not a lot. Mildly unconfident.
5	Neutral. Unsure. Don't know. Indifferent.
6	Sometimes. At times. Moderately. A little bit. Mildly confident.
7	Quite often. A fair bit. Some. A little confident.
8	Most of the time. More often than not. Quite a lot. Quite confident.
9	The majority of the time. A lot. Very confident.
10	Completely. Very much so. A huge amount. Extremely happy. Extremely confident.

Fig. 2 Rate yourself definitions

Top tip

Self-assessment is a vital skill for self-reflection and progression in your professional life. It is important that we are honest, kind and constructive when it comes to self-assessing. It can be easy to be too harsh on yourself when you self-assess and allow your insecurities to cloud your judgement. Being objective and honest about yourself and your practice is a hard thing to do and it takes practice. Before you begin self-assessing, it is important to carefully consider the criteria you are using to assess yourself and focus on that at first without thinking about yourself. Feeling comfortable with what you are assessing will lead to a more accurate assessment. If you jump in and self-assess too early, before you have considered the assessment criteria, you may well have a clouded judgment and be unable to learn as much from the process. Don't rush it – it is too important.

Raising attainment in the classroom: self-assessment questionnaire

QUESTION 1: Does your physical classroom environment promote learning for all?

Quick response:

_____

_____

_____

_____

Questions for consideration

- Have you considered how welcoming the classroom is for children, teachers, other colleagues and parents and carers?
- Have you considered how the learning environment can better support children's learning?
- Have you considered how children can take 'ownership' or have an increased sense of belonging in the learning environment?
- Have you done a needs analysis of how the learning environment could be better used to promote and encourage children's development in maths, literacy and science?

Considered response:

_____

_____

_____

Rate yourself

QUESTION 1: How well does your physical classroom environment promote learning for all?

| 1 | 2 | 3 | 4 | 5 | 6 | 7 | 8 | 9 | 10 |

QUESTION 2: Do you prepare for each task/lesson?

Quick response:

_____

_____

_____

_____

Questions for consideration

- Does your planning start from where the children are in their learning?
- Do you apply aspiration, access and achievement to each child in your planning?
- Does your long-term plan inform your medium-term plan, which in turn informs your short-term plan?

Considered response:

_____

_____

_____

_____

_____

_____

_____

_____

_____

_____

_____

_____

Rate yourself

QUESTION 2: How well do you plan for each task/lesson?

1   2   3   4   5   6   7   8   9   10

QUESTION 3: Do you know your Pupil Premium children?

Quick response:

_____

_____

_____

_____

Questions for consideration

- Do you know who your Pupil Premium children are?
- Do you know their strengths and areas for development?
- Do you closely track their progress in the context of the class, the school, the local area and nationally?

Considered response:

_____

_____

_____

_____

_____

_____

_____

_____

_____

_____

_____

_____

Rate yourself

QUESTION 3: How well do you know your Pupil Premium children?

1	2	3	4	5	6	7	8	9	10

QUESTION 4: Do you know the learning needs of children with SEND?

Quick response:

_____

_____

_____

_____

Questions for consideration

- How quickly do you notice that a child is not making expected progress?
- How quickly do you alter your planning to make changes for their learning?
- How quickly do you implement the changes in your teaching and their learning?
- How often do you informally discuss your concerns with the SENCO?

Considered response:

_____

_____

_____

_____

_____

_____

_____

_____

_____

Rate yourself

QUESTION 4: How well do you know the learning needs of your children with SEND?

1   2   3   4   5   6   7   8   9   10

QUESTION 5: Is assessment part of your daily practice in the classroom?

Quick response:

_____

_____

_____

_____

Questions for consideration

- Are you very familiar with your school's assessment policy?
- Is assessment central to your planning?
- Is assessment part of your classroom practice?

Considered response:

_____

_____

_____

_____

_____

_____

_____

_____

_____

_____

Rate yourself

QUESTION 5: To what extent is assessment part of your daily practice in the classroom?

1   2   3   4   5   6   7   8   9   10

QUESTION 6: Do you use pupil data to consider the impact of your teaching on their learning?

Quick response:

_____

_____

_____

_____

Questions for consideration

- Do you have an effective means of recording pupil data?
- Can you see at a glance how each child is progressing, what they have learnt and where the gaps are?
- How often do you think about your teaching and children's learning in the context of pupil performance data?

Considered response:

_____

_____

_____

_____

_____

_____

_____

_____

_____

Rate yourself

QUESTION 6: To what extent do you use pupil data to consider the impact of your teaching on their learning?

1	2	3	4	5	6	7	8	9	10

QUESTION 7: Are you committed to improving the learning and achievement of every pupil in your class?

Quick response:

_____

_____

_____

_____

Questions for consideration

- How often do you reflect on your subject knowledge and how you will improve any gaps in knowledge?
- How often do you reflect on pedagogy and how you will improve and on the gaps in your classroom practices and approaches?
- Do you consider differentiation for every lesson?

Considered response:

_____

_____

_____

_____

_____

_____

_____

_____

Rate yourself

QUESTION 7: To what extent are you committed to improving the learning and achievement of every pupil in your class?

1   2   3   4   5   6   7   8   9   10

QUESTION 8: Do you plan teaching to achieve progression in pupils' learning?

Quick response:

_____

_____

_____

_____

Questions for consideration

- Do you have clear aims at the beginning of each lesson of what you want children to achieve?
- Do you check pupils have learnt this or part of this after each lesson/activity?
- Do you consider how you can revisit this in the following lesson or through homework or pre-teaching if pupils have not grasped a point?

Considered response:

_____

_____

_____

_____

_____

_____

_____

_____

_____

Rate yourself

QUESTION 8: To what extent do you plan teaching to achieve progression in pupils' learning?

1	2	3	4	5	6	7	8	9	10

QUESTION 9: Do you help children to develop their own learning strategies?

Quick response:

_____

_____

_____

_____

Questions for consideration

- When you are planning do you consider how children learn and incorporate activities accordingly?
- Do you reflect on your teaching after a lesson or at the end of a day, and consider how effective it has been in the context of children's learning?
- Do you regularly give children the opportunity to plan activities in pairs?

Considered response:

_____

_____

_____

_____

_____

_____

_____

_____

_____

Rate yourself

QUESTION 9: To what extent do you support children in developing their own learning strategies?

1   2   3   4   5   6   7   8   9   10

QUESTION 10: Do you work effectively with teaching assistants?

Quick response:

_____

_____

_____

_____

Questions for consideration

- Do you consider teaching assistants' stengths and how these strengths can be used to support children's learning and outcomes?
- Do you plan learning opportunities for an individual child/small group of children to work on with a teaching assistant?
- Do you show the children that the teaching assistant is a valued member of the school community?

Considered response:

_____

_____

_____

_____

_____

_____

_____

_____

_____

Rate yourself

QUESTION 10: How effectively do you work with teaching assistants?

1   2   3   4   5   6   7   8   9   10

QUESTION 11: Do you make provision for wider opportunities for all children?

Quick response:

_____

_____

_____

_____

Questions for consideration

- Do you provide opportunities outside of the classroom for children to develop socially, culturally and personally?
- Do you view extra-curricular activities as a necessary part of education?
- Have you considered your interests/strengths outside of the classroom and how these could be used to start a club for children?

Considered response:

_____

_____

_____

_____

_____

_____

_____

_____

_____

Rate yourself

QUESTION 11: To what extent do you make provision for wider opportunities for all children?

| 1 | 2 | 3 | 4 | 5 | 6 | 7 | 8 | 9 | 10 |

QUESTION 12: Do you engage parents and carers in their children's learning?

Quick response:

_____

_____

_____

_____

Questions for consideration

- Do you involve parents and carers in their child's learning?
- Do you spend time considering how you could involve parents who are not involved in their child's learning?
- Do you consider how you can better engage parents and carers in their child's home learning?

Considered response:

_____

_____

_____

_____

_____

_____

_____

_____

_____

Rate yourself

QUESTION 12: To what extent do you engage parents and carers in their children's learning?

1	2	3	4	5	6	7	8	9	10

QUESTION 13: Do you consider your own personal and professional qualities?

Quick response:

_____

_____

_____

_____

Questions for consideration

- What do you enjoy about your work?
- What do you value in terms of raising the attainment of all children?
- Are these values in line with your school's values?
- Do you use research evidence to investigate your own practice (i.e. your own practical-based research in your classroom or school) with a view to changing your practice?

Considered response:

_____

_____

_____

_____

_____

_____

_____

_____

_____

Rate yourself

QUESTION 13: To what extent do you consider your own personal and professional qualities?

1   2   3   4   5   6   7   8   9   10

The results

Very well done, you have self-evaluated your approach to raising attainment for all children and you are now a step forward in the right direction to gaining expertise in this area. You have considered your personal approach; whether you enjoy it; whether you feel you have impact; the extent to which educational research informs your practice; how well your views fit those of your school; your strengths and weaknesses; what you want to try; and your pupils', parents', carers' and colleagues' thoughts on your approach to raising attainment. It is a lot to take in so take the time to let your self-assessment sink in and reflect on it for a while.

Take a look at how you rated your answers for each question in the questionnaire and compare your ratings with the chart below, which will guide you in taking the next steps in your approach to raising the attainment of every child.

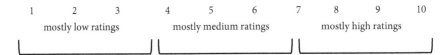

Fig. 3 How did you rate yourself?

Mostly low ratings

You have made an important start. The best starting point for improving practice and raising the attainment of every child is a self-assessment. For each of the 13 areas covered, pick one a week for a term and focus on improving your practice and approach in that area. Make precise and concise notes as you go – more as prompts, to help you make them part of your day-to-day practice.

Mostly medium ratings

You're halfway there. Some of your practices are very good and others are not yet in place. This results in opportunities being lost in the classroom for supporting and helping children to get better outcomes. Identify your three weakest or most challenging areas and think about how you can become an expert. Be honest with yourself. What do you need to do to get better at this practice or approach? Perhaps you need to get better at knowing the research base and doing your own action research or perhaps it is a matter of a sharper focus on aspiration, access and achievement or inclusion in the classroom.

Mostly high ratings

You are already fairly confident in your approaches and practices. You are employing effective approaches and practices to raising children's attainment. You know which children are vulnerable to underachievement and you want to get the best results for them. We never stop learning, changing and improving. Once we are good we want to be great. For each of the 13 areas, consider what you can do in your practice or approach to move from good to great.

Now what?

The results are in. So now what? You have a full and detailed self-reflection on your practices and approach to raising the attainment of every child in your classroom. It is important that you now make the most of it. Take the time to develop an action plan as a result of the answers you have given and the conclusions you have drawn. Don't make this simply another bit of paperwork you have completed. Use it to really open your eyes as to where you are, where you need to be and how to get there. Prioritise what you want to work on and get started.

Chapter 2 takeaway

Teaching tip

You will have discovered from the self-assessment that raising the attainment of every child in your class is about having high expectations for each child, which you make known to them, enabling every child to access learning, using effective teaching strategies and supporting children in developing their own learning strategies. Having done the self-assessment, how would you answer the following questions?

- What strategies do I use to engage children in learning that is meaningful to them?
- What strategies have I used to respond to their learning needs?
- How have I helped the children to develop their own learning strategies?

Pass it on

As a process, self-assessment should inform practice on a day-to-day basis. Effective professional teachers will be effective in their assessment of themselves. In practice, self-assessment will involve making sense of ourselves in the following situations:

Teamwork:	Relationships with:
• listening • attitude • flexibility	• parents • colleagues • children
Knowledge of: • current publications • equal opportunity issues • learning styles	Preparation of: • lessons • monitoring procedures • assessment

Consider the above four categories as a group discussion with colleagues/organise a short CPD session for colleagues. For each one, discuss how you give your best in practice and what you could do better. For each item consider how it impacts on improved outcomes for children. Perhaps at the end of the session, you could develop a general protocol/system to be used across the school.

Share and tweet

Tweet, using the hashtag #BloomsCPD: a self-assessment is the best starting point for raising the attainment of all children in the primary classroom.

CPD book club recommendation

The Tail: How England's Schools Fail One Child in Five – and What Can be Done edited by Paul Marshall

(See bibliography)

This book focuses on the lowest achieving 20 per cent of children, many of whom leave school without the basic skills in literacy and numeracy necessary to gain employment or succeed in life. The strength of the book lies in the way it challenges the reader to think differently, pointing out that with different approaches, practices and cultures in classrooms and schools, teachers can change the trajectories of many of the children who are failed by the system.

Bloggers' corner

The Education Endowment Foundation (EFF) is supported by the government and is looking closely at what works in education to build an evidence base for teachers and leaders of schools and other educational settings.

Available at: www.educationendowmentfoundation.org.uk (go to 'News', then 'Blog').

TO DO LIST:

❑ Make a list of personal and professional learning objectives for the coming term and year and put these into practice (make the focus raising the attainment of every child).

❑ Make a mini action plan of how you are going to achieve these objectives in the time you have allocated.

❑ Organise a CPD session/number of sessions for your colleagues to consider parts of the self- assessment you have just done.

❑ Read *The Tail: How England's Schools Fail One Child in Five – and What Can be Done.*

❑ Look up the blogs on the EEF: www.educationendowmentfoundation. org.uk.

3

Getting to grips with the key researchers

Using evidence-based practice and research studies, not only to inform your practice, but also to change it, has gained momentum over recent years. The reasons for this are clear: it encourages teachers to reflect more deeply on their own practice, consider new ideas for teaching and learning and look beyond their own school. It provides insights into the most effective strategies, gives teachers confidence to try new approaches, is a good form of professional development and leads to improved pupil behaviour, attitudes and attainment (Judkins et al., 2014). Engaging with research improves practice and leads to better pupil outcomes (Handscomb and McBeath, 2003; Cordingley, 2013).

Teachers engaging with research and using it to inform their own practice is supported by the government. This is reflected in the introduction of Teaching Schools in 2011 and the Education Endowment Foundation (EEF) in the same year. The EEF or Sutton Trust is the government's designated What Works Centre for Education. More recently, the Chartered College of Teaching has been formed, which aims to bridge the gap between practice and research.

Any text addressing raising attainment in the primary classroom that did not consider the idea of evidence-based practice would not be doing justice to the subject area. Today we live in a sea of information and filtering out what we can trust can be a challenge. For busy teachers, the situation can be worse; they want to act on reliable and robust evidence and trustworthy claims to knowledge but don't necessarily have the time to evaluate their reliability.

This chapter will show you how to evaluate the evidence and consider some of the influential thinkers in the field along with key organisations you need to consider in developing your practice and improving children's outcomes.

Trusting the evidence

Title: The Sutton Trust Education Endowment Foundation (EEF) Teaching and Learning Toolkit
Available at: https://educationendowmentfoundation.org.uk/evidence-summaries/teaching-learning-toolkit

The Education Endowment Foundation has made research evidence more accessible to teachers. Prior to this, busy teachers often had to refer to lengthy research articles in academic journals, with lengthy conclusions, lacking short and precise summaries. As Sir Kevan Collins said recently:

For years, the worlds of education research and classroom teaching have been too far apart. The EEF's mission has been to make research more accessible to teachers through our Teaching and Learning Toolkit, teacher guidance reports and other resources...' (2018)

The Teaching and Learning Toolkit, widely used by teachers and school leaders, aims to bridge the gap between classroom practice and educational research. In essence, the Toolkit is made up of many summaries of education research studies. Researchers, primarily at Durham University, have looked at large numbers of research studies, identified those that have met their criteria for inclusion and brought the research studies together in a meta-analysis. For example, for the topic of homework (primary), the researchers have looked at all relevant research in this area (according to their criteria for inclusion) and brought the results together to get an overall view of its effectiveness. Each summary:

- provides a definition of the area
- considers how effective it is
- looks at the strength of the evidence they have considered
- considers the costs of implementing it
- discusses what you need to consider before you implement it in your classroom.

You can filter the Toolkit by cost, evidence strength and months of impact on pupil learning outcomes. A printable summary is provided, along with a more detailed report and information about related or ongoing research (funded by the EEF) as well as suggestions for further reading.

This was a major step forward for busy educationalists in terms of time and support. It can be challenging knowing whether the evidence presented in a research journal can be trusted. For example, have the researchers overstated their claim to convince a particular audience? Thankfully, those questions have already been answered by what works centres, like the EEF.

Evaluating other people's work

Not all research is going to be cited on recognised what works centre websites. There will be other research with which teachers engage and they will have to consider the extent to which the research, presented in a journal article, is reliable and robust. Deciding what to accept, because it fits with a predetermined criterion, and what to reject, can have its challenges.

Primarily, it is important to know who the key thinkers are in the chosen area of study and who are the detractors.

Research comes in a variety of forms:

- policy documents
- books
- journal articles (academic research and practitioner)
- reports published by the Department for Education (DfE) or other government agencies
- international reports
- research from recognised what works websites and other websites.

The following questions provide a useful framework when considering the value of a text, whatever form it comes in. They will help you to decide whether you accept a text because it is considered reliable and robust or whether you reject it because the claims it makes are weak or unreliable.

Evaluating the text

- **Why have I selected this text?**
  What do I expect to find? What question am I asking of this text? For example, it may be knowledge or research evidence, etc.
- **What type of literature is this?**
  For example, an article about a piece of research in a school, a policy, a book with facts, etc.
- **Who is the intended audience of this text?**
  For example, have they written it to influence policy-makers, practitioners or students learning a subject, or as a research study/evaluation commissioned by the government? Deciding who the text has been written for helps the researcher to consider how robust the author's argument and supporting evidence might be.
- **What is the text claiming?**
  Consider the conclusions or any assumptions. Have the authors given reasons to support this?
- **How reliable is the supporting evidence of a claim?**
- **If the authors have developed their own framework/concept, how reliable is their claim and what evidence do they have to support this?**
  For example, they might have developed a framework/concept as a means of collecting data.
- **How does the author's values, beliefs and attitudes influence how the findings or conclusions are presented?**
  For example, they may hold a different set of values to your own and make assumptions that you would not necessarily make.
- **To what extent has the author of the text considered the views of his or her critics and provided a defence?**

- **How do the claims fit with your experience?**
  For example, do they resonate with you, surprise you or otherwise?
- **Overall, having read the text and in the light of your research question/aim, how reliable are the claims made?**
  This includes having read key sections, e.g. conclusions including reasons given for this, introductions including rationale to support that and executive summaries.

(Adapted from Poulson and Wallace, 2004)

Raising attainment in the primary classroom: the research

Having considered current research evidence bases and how you critique a piece of text, the following section gives you pointers towards current research that can be trusted and on which you can expand through the recommended websites.

Teaching and learning

High-quality teaching and learning is based on the belief that teachers and school leaders can have a profound impact on all pupils by developing their achievement, access and aspirations. This does not happen by chance. In high-performing education systems across OECD (Organisation for Economic Co-operation and Development) countries, teacher professional development is both collective and more central to pupil performance; improvement across the system is through 'conscious, deliberate and sustained effort' (Truss, 2014). It is based on teachers, pupils and their parents knowing where the children are in their learning, where they are aiming to get and how to get there. It is founded on collaborative working, active learning and teachers constantly reflecting on how they can get better at it. In practice, it means:

For teachers:

- knowing your pupils and how they learn
- having high aspirations for their learning
- giving children a sense of ownership of learning
- taking a more personalised approach to children's learning
- keeping good records.

For pupils:

- being able to access the curriculum
- having teachers who raise their aspirations and increase their achievements

- having confidence in their own capabilities
- having high self-esteem
- developing self-mastery skills.

For parents:

- knowing where their child is in their learning
- knowing how to support them in their learning
- having high aspirations for their learning and achievement.

(Source: Blandford and Knowles, 2013)

Key research

This section considers some of the research evidence relating to what makes great teaching and how, when it is effectively implemented, developed and embedded, it can raise the attainment of every child.

Title: What makes great teaching? Review of the underpinning research

Authors: Robert Coe, Cesare Aloisi, Steve Higgins and Lee Elliot Major

Year: 2014

Format: Report

Available at: https://www.suttontrust.com/wp-content/uploads/2014/10/What-Makes-Great-Teaching-REPORT.pdf

---

Summary

Coe et al. list six common elements of quality teaching suggested by research evidence:

- content knowledge (pedagogical)
- quality of instruction
- classroom climate
- classroom management
- teacher beliefs
- professional behaviour.

In practice these are borne out differently in the classroom and across the school; the synergy between the elements is a key consideration. Teacher beliefs – the reasons why you adopt particular practices and theories about learning – can be a central area for reflection. For example, by changing your level of aspiration for pupils you can adapt your established beliefs and behaviours; this can result in pupils with higher aspirations and better outcomes. Encouraging teachers to develop themselves, deepening their subject knowledge and learning to use it as effectively as possible, is self-evident. What can be lacking is a focus on the synergy between the other elements of quality teaching and the extent to which you as a teacher 'take ownership' for change.

What you need to consider

An effective teacher will demonstrate all these elements in their teaching. In practice, it means thinking in advance and planning. The following provides pointers for you to think about in advance:

- **Content knowledge (pedagogical)**: reflect on areas of a subject that you do not know well and look them up; consider how children will assimilate what you are teaching, including perceived 'difficult' areas and how you will teach them so that all children learn.
- **Quality of instruction**: consider the focus. Could you take it to a higher level? E.g. critique a piece of writing. Also consider scaffolding and the types of questions you will ask children to move them forward in their learning.
- **Classroom climate**: consider how you show children that you have high aspirations for their learning and outcomes, including showing that 'successes' depend on effort and not ability.
- **Classroom management**: consider the resources you will use and know how to use them effectively, how you will teach the children to use them and how you manage behaviour for learning.
- **Teacher beliefs**: consider your teaching practices and why you might 'do it' this way and not that way; what has influenced your beliefs and values?
- **Professional behaviour**: consider how you relate to and support children and how effectively you model behaviour, including your interaction with colleagues, parents and carers and the wider community.

Read the introduction of this report, which provides a summary of the key points about each of the six elements of quality teaching. For each one, consider what is your 'takeaway' sentence. And for each one consider where you are now in your professional knowledge and classroom practice and what you could do to make that even better.

Title: *Inside the Black Box: Raising Standards Through Classroom Assessment*
Authors: Paul Black and Dylan Wiliam
Year: 1998
Format: Book
Publisher: GL Assessment

Summary

Advances in the theory and practice of effective assessment owe much to the groundbreaking work in the late 1990s of the Assessment Reform Group (ARG). The aim of the ARG was to: ' ... ensure that assessment policy and practice at all levels takes account of relevant research evidence' (Nuffield Foundation). As part of the ARG, a major review of the research literature on the assessment of pupils and young people's learning was undertaken by Paul Black and Dylan Wiliam in 1996. The review found extensive evidence that 'formative assessment' could improve learning and could deepen pupils' and young people's learning and achievement. Their research led to the development of a framework that they called Assessment for Learning, which, if implemented in practice, enables children to know where they are in their learning, where they are going and how to get there. It is based on the following ten principles, which provide a framework for good practice in assessment for raising attainment. For each one consider how you do it and how you could do it better:

- helps learners know how to improve
- engages children in self-assessment
- is central to effective planning
- addresses how children learn
- is crucial to classroom practice
- is a professional skill
- is sensitive and constructive
- fosters motivation
- promotes understanding of objectives
- recognises educational achievement. *(Adapted from ARG, 2002)*

What you need to consider

Reflect on the following, which will support you in developing the above framework in your classroom, making it part of daily practice:

- Consider how you show children what their strengths are in a piece of work and the extent to which you give children further opportunities to improve on any weaknesses.
- Consider the extent to which, and how, you provide children with the opportunity to assess their own work and identify what they know and do not know and what they need to do to fill the gaps in their learning.
- Consider the extent to which your planning includes opportunities for children's 'new' ideas to be further explored in the classroom, and consider the extent to which you make children aware of how they will be assessed and the criteria for assessment.
- Consider the extent to which you enable children to know the 'how' of learning – that is, providing the opportunity for children to talk to each other about their learning.

- Consider the extent to which you integrate a learning opportunity into day-to-day practice, because you have observed something new or unexpected in a child's learning.
- Consider how you feed back to children. Is it motivating and focused on their efforts?
- Consider the extent to which and how you 'reward' children's successes. Also consider the following trusted websites.

Other relevant websites

- **Research Schools Network (EEF/IEE)**

  Research schools support other schools within their network in using research evidence to inform practice. They also support teacher research. The network is a collaboration between the Education Endowment Foundation and the Institute of Effective Education. You will find the website useful for the latest research and training events.

  Available at: https://educationendowmentfoundation.org.uk/ scaling-up-evidence/research-schools/

- **Teaching Schools Council**

  The Teaching Schools Council is a national organisation with over 20 members, which provides an advisory and regulatory body for the 800 Teaching Schools across the country. You will find its publications useful for improving your practice in the context of raising attainment.

  Available at: https://www.tscouncil.org.uk/

- Research publications and projects that support school improvement in teaching school are available at: https://www.gov.uk/government/collections/ teaching-schools-national-research-and-development

  These include publications on closing the gap, evidence-based teaching, joint practice development and school-based research on pedagogy.

- **British Educational Research Association (BERA)**
  BERA aims to improve research quality and encourage engagement in and with research. The BERA journal publishes high-quality educational research and, through its publications, aims to inform both policy and practice. You will find the website useful for looking at the latest research news.

  Available at: https://www.bera.ac.uk/

- **The Chartered College of Teaching**

  The Chartered College of Teaching was set up in 2016 and took its first members in 2017. Its aim is to increase the professional status of teachers in

England and improve the professional framework for teaching. You will find the Chartered College blogs useful, as well as the latest news.

Available at: https://chartered.college/

Structured approaches to engaging parents in their child's learning

A review of the literature highlights the complexity in either clearly defining parental support or 'distilling' the effect from other variables. However, Gorard et al. (2012), in their review of related literature, cite 'parent as teacher and parent–school alignment' as the two principal mechanisms through which parental involvement impacts on children's attainment. Harris and Goodall (2007) highlight the nature of parental *engagement*, which 'is not about engaging with the school, but with the learning of the child' (p. 37) and where 'engagement implies that parents are an essential part of the learning process, an extended part of the pedagogic process' (p. 67). And it is on this area that teachers need to focus.

Key research

Title: Review of best practice in parental engagement

Authors: Janet Goodall and John Vorhaus, with Jon Carpentieri, Greg Brooks, Rodie Akerman and Alma Harris

Year: 2011

Format: Research paper

Available at: https://www.education.gov.uk/publications/RSG/publicationDetail/Page1/DFE-RR156

Summary

This research report presents a review of studies aimed at supporting and improving parental engagement in the education of children aged five to 19; educational outcomes are considered. The researchers reviewed UK studies carried out between 2000 and 2010; earlier studies that were frequently cited were included, as were authoritative and relevant international studies. A total of 1,200 titles were reviewed. The results are presented over the following three areas:

1. **School–home links:** findings showed that schools need a whole approach to engaging parents in their child's learning, where teachers receive training to do this effectively and initiatives to engage parents consider the context (there is no one approach for all); the most effective approaches involved parents receiving very clear and specific information and two-way communication (parents letting teachers know about what their child was doing out of school).
2. **Support and training for parents and family**: findings showed strong evidence of the impact of parent training programmes on children's literacy. Schools that were effective in engaging parents in their child's learning focused on certain groups of parents and started with a needs analysis.
3. **Community-based interventions**: findings showed the very positive impact on children's learning and outcomes when their family (parents/carers) were engaged in family literacy, language and numeracy programmes.

What you need to think about

Look closely at how the researchers carried out the research process. Was their methodological approach to data collection reliable? Why? Reflect on the following summary adapted from the review of evidence in the report; in particular, consider how the researchers developed the three themes over which they presented the results. What is it about their research approach and presentation of findings that makes the report reliable?

School–home links

- Whole-school approach needed.
- Staff need training.
- Parental engagement strategies need to relate to the context of the school.
- Parental engagement must be a two-way exchange of knowledge and understanding: school to home and home to school.
- Using ICT supports parental engagement.
- Challenges for parents can include cost, time and transport. Challenges for teachers can include not collecting sufficient data on their interventions.

Support and training for parents

- Effective programmes have an impact on how well children become involved in school.
- They have a positive impact on children's literacy (e.g. by teaching parents to teach specific reading skills to their children).
- Effective programmes are initiated through a needs analysis.
- There is a need to understand what parents already do with their children.

Family and community-based interventions

- Family literacy, language and numeracy programmes have a positive impact on children's academic and learning outcomes.
- Multi-agency arrangements are essential for sharing information.
- Schools need to share information when children move.
- Challenges include a lack of data-sharing.

Reflect on parental engagement in your school in light of these results. Could you do it better? Is there any aspect of parental engagement you would like to research in your classroom/school? Some of the above details should prompt the types of research questions you would like to explore. How would you go about doing the research?

Wider outcomes and opportunities

In many schools in England, wider provision is often seen as an 'add-on' to the main curriculum and can be relatively underdeveloped. In an age when great emphasis is placed on academic outcomes, extra-curricular or enrichment activities can be seen as less important. Yet it is the extra-curricular activities that not only contribute to better academic outcomes, but also help to build resilience, confidence and self-esteem in children and young people. The scant research available in this area and mainly from relatively small-scale studies shows that when children engage in wider activities they have higher academic achievement. Enrichment activities provided by schools – for example, sport, music, debating and chess – are particularly beneficial to children's social and emotional development (Yeo and Graham, 2015).

Key research

The following research reports are useful to consider:

Title: Life lessons: improving essential life skills for young people

Authors: Carl Cullinane and Rebecca Montacute

Available at: https://www.suttontrust.com/wp-content/uploads/2017/10/Life-Lessons-Report_FINAL.pdf

---

Title: Understanding 'soft skills' development at independent schools: an analysis of mental toughness at UK independent schools

Published by: AQR International

Available at: https://www.isc.co.uk/media/3856/isc_soft_skills_mental_toughness_report.pdf

Title: A deep dive into social and emotional learning: what do the views of those involved tell us about the challenges for policy-makers?

Authors: Alice Yeo and Jenny Graham

Available at: https://www.gov.uk/government/uploads/system/uploads/attachment_data/file/411493/A_deep_dive_into_social_and_emotional_learning._What_do_the_views_of_those_involved_tell_us_about_the_challenges_for_policy-makers.pdf

Summary

'Life lessons: improving essential life skills for young people' shows that 'life skills' like the development of confidence, social skills, self-control, motivation and resilience are as important to lifelong learning as academic subjects; these particular characteristics are considered to contribute to a child's success in school and beyond. This report explores the extent to which teachers and employers consider them to be important and concludes that there is increasing recognition of their centrality to success in school and life and the need for children to develop them at school. Findings showed that 88 per cent of young people, 94 per cent of employers and 97 per cent of teachers believe that 'life skills' are as or more important than academic qualifications.

In 'Understanding "soft skills" development at independent schools', the researchers explore the development of soft skills (control, commitment, challenge and confidence) and mental toughness in 9,000 pupils at independent schools in England and Scotland. Using a mental toughness test, the findings showed that pupils at independent schools (those belonging to the Independent Schools Council) have good attainment, wellbeing and behaviour and can deal with setbacks; they concluded that this made the pupils more open to learning.

In 'A deep dive into social and emotional learning', researchers explored how children and young people learn social and emotional skills in education and the youth sector. Findings showed that there is variability in 'if' and 'how' children and young people are taught these skills. The authors concluded that further research was needed into what effective provision should 'look like' in practice. They believe that without this, provision may not focus enough on enabling children and young people to develop these skills and learn how to cope with challenging situations.

What you need to think about

Provision of wider opportunities enables pupils to become involved in the whole life of the school. Reflect on the key points in these reports, particularly focusing on the introduction, executive summaries and conclusions. What extra-curricular activities or clubs do you provide for your class? It can be helpful to think about how you would implement and develop wider opportunities. One of the four elements of the Achievement for All framework for schools enables schools to focus on the development of wider opportunities, and in so doing they can:

- improve attendance
- improve behaviour
- eliminate bullying
- enable children to develop positive relationships with others
- increase children's participation in all aspects of the school life, particularly extra-curricular activities (Blandford and Knowles, 2013).

Leading learning

Research shows that children and young people from less advantaged families often do not do as well at school and throughout their education as their more advantaged peers. For some children the educational gap that opens even before they start school may never close. It does not have to be like this. As we have shown in this book, with the right approach, inspirational teachers and teaching and a supportive culture, the gap can be closed and all children can achieve well at school. The following report considers further examples of classroom practices that contribute to this.

Key research

Title: Supporting the attainment of disadvantaged pupils: articulating success and good practice

Authors: Shona Macleod, Caroline Sharp, Daniele Bernardinelli, et al.

Year: 2015

Format: Research report

Available at: https://www.gov.uk/government/uploads/system/uploads/attachment_data/file/473974/DFE-RR411_Supporting_the_attainment_of_disadvantaged_pupils.pdf

Summary

In November 2014, the Department for Education commissioned the National Foundation for Educational Research (NfER) to investigate the differences between schools in the performance of pupils from disadvantaged backgrounds.

The aims were to:

- Identify any common features of schools that had narrowed the gap successfully.
- Identify any possible groups/clusters of schools that had narrowed the gap, and why.
- Consider what schools that had narrowed the gap were doing compared to other schools.

Overall findings showed that schools had used a relatively large number of different strategies to close the gap. Those schools that were more successful in raising the attainment of disadvantaged pupils viewed it within the context of a school-wide policy and approach to raise the attainment of all pupils. They had an inclusive approach and demonstrated clear leadership of learning. The most successful schools had the following characteristics:

- a culture of attainment for all pupils
- identified and addressed pupil barriers to learning early
- focused on high-quality teaching in the classroom
- a focus on pupil outcomes
- the best teachers, who knew the pupils well, taught the less advantaged children.

They knew the pupils well through regular checking and tracking of data and made decisions accordingly. They had clear leadership, with high aspirations for all children, and gave 'ownership' of raising attainment to all staff (leaders of learning in the classroom).

What you need to think about

Look up the report and reflect on the key strategies:

- Which worked well?
- Why did they work?

Then consider, as a leader of learning within your classroom:

- What could you do better to raise the attainment of your Pupil Premium children?

Engaging with research

The following books will help you to think about how to engage with research more. Research in education was given impetus in England with the publication of Ben Goldacre's (2013) report for the Department for Education, 'Building evidence into education'. A medical doctor by profession, he highlighted the need for evidence-based practice in teaching, which should begin during initial teacher training. So often, he states, teacher training presents the results of research as a 'completed canon of answers' without students being taught to critique the research, considering the different methods used and the strengths and weaknesses of each. 'Learning the basics of how research works is important', he states, 'not because every teacher should be a researcher, but because it allows teachers to be critical consumers of the new research findings that will come out during the many decades of their career.' (pp. 16-17)

This section outlines a number of good books that you can refer to, to improve your own knowledge of the research process to become a 'critical consumer'.

Title: *Research Methods in Education*
Authors: Louis Cohen, Lawrence Manion and Keith Morrison
Year: 2017
Format: Book
Publisher: Routledge

Now in its eighth edition, this book is considered one of the main standard texts for doing research. This book will enable you to think about the whole process and better identify the issue, the sample and the best method to use; much research uses a mixed method approach (using multiple ways to explore the research question, both quantitative and qualitative approaches).

Title: *Qualitative Research for Education: An Introduction to Theories and Methods*
Authors: Robert Bogdan and Sari Knopp Biklin
Year: 2007
Format: Book
Publisher: Pearson

This book provides an introduction to all aspects of qualitative research. It will enable you to look at your research questions and consider what is the best approach to help you answer them. The book is set within a sociological context, which is what qualitative research is about. It has a section on ten common questions about qualitative research, which provides a useful guide for considering whether you employ a qualitative approach to your research.

Title: *Becoming Critical: Education Knowledge and Action Research*
Authors: Stephen Kemmis and Wilfred Carr
Year: 1986
Format: Book
Publisher: Deakin University Press

Learning to critique other research is an important part of your own research. When you look at a research report, you will want to know whether you can accept the results as good evidence or not. This process in itself will enable you to plan a more reliable and robust approach to collecting and analysing your own data. *Becoming Critical* supports you in doing that. Focused on action research, the book provides a good foundation on the background of research and how the particular perspective of the researcher will influence how the results are presented.

Other useful websites for improving practice and raising attainment include:

- National Association for Primary Education: http://nape.org.uk/
- Nursery World: https://www.nurseryworld.co.uk/
- Achievement for All (Bubble): https://afaeducation.org/

Chapter 3 takeaway

Teaching tip

Identify an area of your practice you would like to change. Look up some of the existing research in the field. Select one research study that you feel is noteworthy. Analyse it; what does it show? Use what you have learnt in this chapter.

Pass it on

Bring together a group of colleagues and present your selected research paper. Set it within the context of why you think it is worthy of note. Open it up to discussion.

Share and tweet

Using the series hashtag #BloomsCPD, share the new insights into identifying reliable and robust evidence you have learnt in this chapter

CPD book club recommendation

Research Methods in Education by Louis Cohen, Lawrence Manion and Keith Morrison

(See bibliography)

This book is considered one of the main standard texts for doing research.

Bloggers' corner

The EEF have regular blogs on current research and policy. An interesting blog to read is that by Sally Fox, 'Driving school improvement' (1 February 2018).

Available at: https://chartered.college/guest-blog-driving-school-improvement

TO DO LIST:

- ❏ Look up all of the recommended books in this chapter and read the summaries in each chapter. Is there an area you need to further develop? Read about that area in more detail.
- ❏ Browse the Chartered College of Teaching blogs available at https://chartered.college/category/blog.
- ❏ Read Sally Fox's blogpost 'Driving school improvement'.
- ❏ Reflect on how you could better use research evidence to inform your practice.
- ❏ Discuss with colleagues how you could further develop this collaboratively.

4 Overview of the main strategies

This chapter is about how you build the core in children:

- Aspiration: *I can*
- Access: *I do*
- Attainment: *I have*
- Achievement: *I am*

First we will look in more detail at these foundational stones of raising attainment for all and the centrality of developing the core in children. Effective systems encourage aspiration and provide pupils with support to achieve better outcomes, enable every pupil to access learning opportunities, welcome parents as valued partners and value all children.

We will then develop these ideas, enabling you to become a better leader in the classroom and in leading others across the school, by providing an overview of key strategies you can use. We'll show how inclusive classrooms are developed by rethinking approaches and building on strengths and potential, and how this enhances practice.

Strategies include:

- structured approaches to engaging parents/carers and children
- systems to track and measure progress
- staff with good levels of knowledge of special educational needs
- how to address the needs of students vulnerable to underachievement
- suitable teaching approaches (Quality Teaching and Learning)
- differentiated teaching to meet individual needs
- the use of interventions at the appropriate time.

Laying the foundations

Aspiration, access and achievement should be applied to all children and young people. A recent study by Achievement for All and KPMG of good practice in primary and early years maths found that primary schools that are getting it right ensure that children likely to underachieve are exposed to the same rich maths experiences as their peers; if they fail to grasp a concept in one lesson, they spend a short time with the teacher going over it before the next lesson. Focused teacher CPD was a central characteristic in these schools (Knowles, 2017). Teachers are leaders in their classroom and have the freedom to rethink practices and make changes. Often, what is needed is new thinking to answer old questions (Blandford, 2017).

Applying aspiration, access and achievement

The interconnectedness of aspiration, access and achievement is reflected in the following diagram.

Aspiration includes, but is not limited to:

- motivation
- orientation
- self-concept and self-efficacy.

Access includes, but is not limited to:

- engagement
- barriers of exclusion
- opportunity and participation.

Achievement includes, but is not limited to:

- attainment
- experience of success and progress.

Achievement *includes but is not limited to:*
-attainment,
-experience of success,
-progress.

Access *includes but is not limited to:*
-engagement,
-exclusionary barriers,
-opportunity,
-participation.

Aspiration *includes but is not limited to:*
-motivation,
-orientation,
-self-concept,
-self-efficacy.

Fig. 4 Aspiration, access and achievement

Aspiration

Aspiration is about having high expectations in relation to what children can achieve; this includes teachers, practitioners, parents, carers and other professionals. For children, it is the 'I can': their aspirations will be reflected in a 'can do' mentality, displayed when they decide to meet challenges and gain access to learning, thus believing that they can succeed (Blandford and Knowles, 2013). Pupil motivation, however, can be affected by a number of factors including socio-economic disadvantage and SEND; parental engagement has a very distinct and wide-reaching effect on pupil aspirations and motivation. Parents with low aspirations often unintentionally pass their beliefs and feelings on to their children. It is important that pupils from less advantaged families and those with SEND feel motivated, not only to overcome potential barriers but also to continue to have aspirations about what they are able to achieve. This is promoted and encouraged when an aspirational outlook is developed in the classroom, with systems in place to support it.

In order for pupils to become aspirational in the school environment or to continue to raise their aspirations, it is crucial for teachers and other staff to be aspirational for them. Without a culture that models aspirational values and holds a strong belief in the pupils' abilities to access and achieve, it is difficult for them to do so. A pupil's mindset can greatly affect their desire to access school, achieve and improve their future. Pupils can be disengaged or negative for a number of reasons, ranging from established family views about education to their previous experiences in school.

Access

Access is the 'I do' for children and young people and in practice has a two-fold meaning. The first is the removal of barriers preventing access to learning; these can be broad or specific – for example, low expectations, physiological, social, environmental, educational barriers and more. The second meaning is the provision of education, compulsory, further and higher, and for those who might not have previously perceived education as having any significance or value in their lives.

Achievement

Achievement, on the other hand, is the internalisation of learning and success; for children and young people, the 'I am'. In many ways it has been devalued by the political drive to 'count' examination results as the single indicator of educational success or attainment. Whilst it is essential that the workforce is literate and numerate, knowing what achievement is, having the self-efficacy to achieve and recognising when this happens is fundamental to learning. Achievement lies within and extends beyond exams: social, artistic, musical, sporting and leadership endeavours all count towards the achievement of all. It is the breadth of success that facilitates the application of learning.

Inclusion

The role of the teacher is fundamental in fostering understanding of inclusive thinking and practice in the classroom and educational community. In doing so, it is necessary to have an understanding regarding the opinions, attitudes and experiences of colleagues, parents and carers, and children. Good conditions for learning and development recognise that to achieve the highest standards and sustain improvement, social interactions, the curriculum (both formal and informal) and the other learning experiences of the child should be considered as a whole. In 2015, the Centre for Studies on Inclusive Education (drawing on the work of Booth and Ainscow, 2011) explained what inclusion in education means:

- 'Putting inclusive values into action.
- Viewing every life and every death as of equal worth.
- Supporting everyone to feel that they belong.
- Increasing participation for children and adults in learning and teaching activities, relationships and communities of local schools.
- Reducing exclusion, discrimination, and barriers to learning and participation.
- Restructuring cultures, policies and practices to respond to diversity in ways that value everyone equally.
- Linking education to local and global realities.
- Learning from the reduction of barriers for some children, to benefit children more widely.
- Viewing differences between children and between adults as resources for learning.
- Acknowledging the right of children to an education of high quality in their locality.
- Improving schools for staff and parents/carers as well as children.
- Emphasising the development of school communities and values, as well as achievements.
- Fostering mutually sustaining relationships between schools and surrounding communities.
- Recognising that inclusion in education is one aspect of inclusion in society.'

(Source: Centre for Studies on Inclusive Education, 2015)

Creating an inclusive learning context is not to be viewed or understood as an end point or conclusion. It is not a product that emerges when a teacher or educational community employs a particular formula for the management of teaching and learning. Nor is it a restrictive, bounded scientific theory. Rather, inclusive thinking and practice results in a process of constant development where decisions are made and actions taken on the basis of the inclusion of all.

Developing the core

There is no evidence that the attainment gap cannot be closed. It is a matter of changing the way we think, act and engage – and crucial for teachers. At the foundation of any effective framework within an inclusive educational environment is the development of the core: *I can, I do, I have* and *I am*.

- **Aspiration, 'I can':** the grit and resilience that makes perseverance in the face of challenge a 'lived practice' of children and young people, understanding and supporting learning, building ambition and goal-focused behaviour.
- **Access, 'I do':** developing independence in learning and self-development in children and young people, leading to an understanding and ownership of their responsibility for their own ongoing lifelong journey of learning and development.
- **Attainment, 'I have':** attaining the grade – 'I have passed'.
- **Achievement, 'I am':** the internalisation of learning and success, the 'feel good' factor of learning that grows from within, equipping children and young people to understand what they know and how to learn. (Blandford, 2017)

Structured approaches to engaging parents/carers and children

There is a strong association between parental support of children's education and their academic achievement, as we have discussed previously in this book. For some parents and carers, this can seem like a daunting task and for others, they think it is the responsibility of the school. Teachers are then left with the dilemma of considering what practical steps can be taken to guide and encourage parents to support their children's learning at home.

One possible solution is to take a structured approach. This can start with a simple analysis of parents who are engaged – in what ways and why? – and parents who are not engaged and why, taking into consideration the context of your school. From this simple analysis, solutions of how you can better engage parents will start to emerge. But it is worth considering that, for some parents, this might involve a step-by-step approach – liaison, engagement and finally partnership.

Initial practical approaches can include encouraging parents and carers to read with or to their children or talk to them, asking their views on certain happenings/issues or sending home maths bags with five-minute activities for parents and children to do together. Some parents would like to do these activities but do not know how to start. Encouraging parents to become engaged through parent or carer and children's workshops, showing them what their child is doing in literacy or maths or science and how they can support that at home, can make a big difference. The following section takes this a step further and considers what we mean by parent and carer engagement and how this can be developed through the structured conversation model employed by Achievement for All.

Teachers: what to do in practice

Harris and Goodall (2007, pp. 37, 67) highlight the nature of parental **engagement**, which 'is not about engaging with the school, but with the learning of the child' and where 'engagement implies that parents are an essential part of the learning process, an extended part of the pedagogic process'. And it is on this latter area that teachers focus.

For parents, structured conversations (a structured two-way discussion between parents or carers, the teacher and their child) provide a forum to engage with the school, and speak about their child's interests and learning and their aspirations for their child. This model, pioneered in the Achievement for All programme, provides an opportunity to involve parents in their child's learning and to discuss and set their targets together. It is an opportunity to enhance and further develop their aspirations and to communicate this to their child. For schools, structured conversations provide time to listen to parents, talk to parents about their children's learning and reflect upon ways to transfer this to the classroom. In practice, it involves teachers initially identifying a group of pupils who would benefit, contacting the parents and arranging a discussion time for parents to come into the school to talk about their child and his/her learning and interests. Evidence shows that one a term is effective (PwC, 2015 and 2016).

This is reflected in the comments made by parents of children with SEND who participated in the Achievement for All pilot:

- 'I feel listened to and really valued in the structured conversations.' (Year 5 parent)

- 'I know exactly what type of support my son is receiving and what his targets are so that I can help him more too.' (Year 5 parent)

In successful structured conversations:

- The teacher, the parents/carers and the child are involved.
- Other professionals involved are invited to join part of the consultation by the parents/carers.
- The teacher shapes the consultation.
- Parents/carers are full partners in any decisions.
- Parents/carers are given information rather than advice.

Effective preparation by teachers:

- Involves personal invitation to the parents or carers.
- Involves clarity about who will be at the consultation from the school or other agencies (e.g. if a child has an additional need, a speech therapist might be present or if English is not the first language of the parent, a translator may be present).
- Lets parents/carers know how much time has been allocated for the consultation.
- Considers childcare arrangements for younger siblings.
- Includes a small number of questions for parents to consider to help them to be ready for the consultation.
- Offers parents an advocate (e.g. from Parent Partnership Service) or allows them to bring a friend or family member as a supporter.

Systems to track and measure progress

In principle, systems to track and measure progress are needed to get the best outcomes for the child. Effective tracking systems enable teachers, children and their parents or carers to work together to assess 'where the learners are in their learning, where they need to go and how best to get there' (ARG, 2002).

Since the introduction of life without levels, there has been stronger emphasis on learning and development as meeting the individual needs of the child through ongoing observation and assessment or formative assessment – which Shepard et al. (2005, p. 275) define as 'assessment carried out during the instructional process for the purpose of improving teaching or learning'. Formative assessment informs a continuous process of observation, feedback, evaluation and progress. The Final report of the commission on assessment without levels (Crown, 2015) gave the key purposes of formative assessment as:

- allowing teachers to understand pupil performance on a continuing basis.
- enabling teachers to identify when pupils are struggling, when they have consolidated learning and when they are ready to progress.
- supporting teachers to provide appropriate support or extension as necessary.
- enabling teachers to evaluate their own teaching of particular topics or concepts and to plan future lessons accordingly.

(Crown, 2015, p. 19)

Formative assessment will inform teaching and learning, but

> 'Summative assessment sums up what a pupil has achieved at the end of a period of time, relative to the learning aims and the relevant national standards... There may be an assessment at the end of a topic, at the end of a term or half-term, at the end of a year... A summative assessment may be a written test, an observation, a conversation or a task.' (NfER, 2007, p. 1)

Summative assessment is an important aspect of the assessment process, which also informs data-led discussions around pupil learning and attainment.

Teachers: what to do in practice

Overall and Sangster (2006, p. 75) suggest that 'for formative assessment to be successful it is about creating a classroom in which children become engaged in learning which is meaningful to them and you and they have strategies to respond to their learning needs'.

In practice, this is a cyclical process, which informs long-, medium- and short-term planning. Effective assessment involves gathering and analysing the evidence of children's learning and allowing time to reflect on how you will use this evidence to develop children's learning priorities and/or targets. The following framework, developed as a set of questions, will help you to do this.

Consider:

1. **What aspect of learning do I want to assess?** For example, pre-testing before a module to find out the strengths and weaknesses of a child's knowledge and understanding.
2. **What is the best way of collecting this data?** For example, observation, written test, discussion, group activity.
3. **What am I looking for?**
4. **What does it tell me about the child?**
5. **What aspects do I need to consider to support this child's learning/progress?**

6. **How much time do I need to give this child to develop this skill/progress in this area?**

On a daily basis you will be collecting evidence of children's learning through both formal and informal interaction with them. Short-term plans, perhaps developed on a weekly basis, should be flexible enough to take into account daily planned, unplanned and impromptu happenings that may provide new insights into a child's learning. Short-term plans, however, will include prompts indicating to you:

- when to collect evidence about a child's learning
- what you are looking for
- what questions you might ask the child
- how you will ask the question
- when you might intervene with a question or a comment
- whether you will scaffold learning
- what you will do to move that child forward in his/her learning.

They will also include notes to indicate how you are going to alter your teaching to take into account any new evidence of learning.

Data should be recorded (using the school system) and discussed regularly at data discussion meetings. Discussion needs to revolve around:

- the child's progress
- his/her performance against expectation
- his/her performance within the context of the school, the local authority or across a MAT and nationally
- possible strategies to move the child forward in his/her learning.

In summary, it means collecting the right data by developing a grid to record attainment (develop a personal grid for your class), setting meaningful targets for each pupil, analysing the data (at class, school, local and national level), more frequently analysing data at class level, identifying gaps in progress and attainment for each pupil and reflecting on how you can address them, involving parents and carers in that process, planning, implementing, monitoring, evaluating and using ICT effectively to support the process (being confident in the use of school tracking systems).

Staff with good levels of knowledge of special educational needs (SEN)

Early identification of a learning need, along with early action, is vital to prevent any further delay in the child making progress. This is why it is important for staff to have a good level of knowledge of SEN. The Code of Practice (DfE/DoH, 2015) is clear: all teaching should be high quality, with careful monitoring of progress and carefully planned interventions. When this is in place, identification of any learning needs will be more efficient. You should consider:

- Do you act quickly if you think a child is not making expected progress?
- Do you feel your identification of a SEN is timely and appropriate?
- Do you consult regularly with your SENCO about your practice for children identified with SEND?
- Do you keep an evidence trail, which is important if the Education Health and Care Plan process formally begins?

Teachers: what to do in practice

Teachers should use the four-stage *graduated approach:*

1. Assess
2. Plan
3. Do
4. Review

This four-stage approach with evidence of progress should be used to inform next steps. This evidence trail is important when or if an Education Health Care Plan (EHC Plan) process formally begins.

When a school makes special educational provision for a child with SEN, the school must inform the parents. This process is led and co-ordinated by the SENCO, who supports teachers. The principles of early support do enable a fast-track process should serious concerns regarding special needs be noted. Figure 5 on page 60 outlines the graduated response in practice.

In practice, you notice a child is not making expected progress. As a result you:

- Make adjustments in your planning to support the child in making the progress you expect (how will you remove their barriers to learning? Consider what one extra activity/resource/other you could put in place that will help the child make progress).
- Implement the adjustments into your classroom practice (remove their barriers to learning).
- Monitor the child closely within a reasonable timeframe you set (observe, question, prompt and monitor the data). At this stage you can also speak to the SENCO about it and discuss your plan (this will be an informal discussion, but you should keep a record of it).
- If the child has made the progress you expect, maintain 'normal' classroom provision.

- If the child has not made the progress you expect, talk to the SENCO (and keep a record of this).
- The SENCO will assess the child and will plan further interventions to help the child make progress.
- You will implement and monitor the interventions with the support of the SENCO.
- With the SENCO, you will decide if the child has made expected progress.
- If the child has not made the expected progress, the EHC assessment process begins and you will be supported by the SENCO.

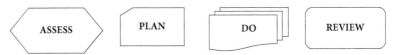

✳ The dotted arrow indicates fast-track early intervention if needs are significant

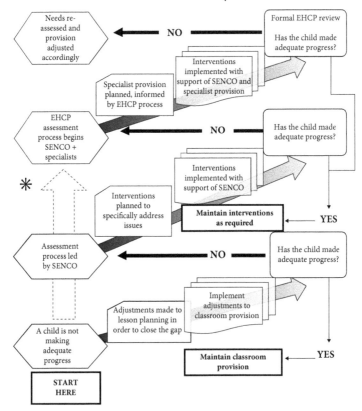

Fig. 5 The graduated flowchart   (Source: Achievement for All, 2015)

How to address the needs of pupils at risk of underachievement

Barriers to a child's progress arise from a complex interplay of factors, including attitudes, values, experiences and practices existing at the child's social, biological, developmental and educational level. Schools can change this. Schools help when children have supportive teachers whose morale is high and are provided with creative extracurricular activities (OECD, 2016). In practice this means teachers are available for support and teaching, are willing to see the learner's perspective on work problems, are willing to support the learner's competencies and will challenge the learner to be active and responsible in choosing, planning, executing and evaluating the activity and its outcomes.

Scaffolding is a fundamental pedagogy for supporting the child or young person, to help them build on their previous knowledge and learn new information, in order to achieve the intended outcome of the activity (based on the Vygotskian concept of the *zone of proximal development* (ZPD).

For those at risk of underachievement, a lot of work in the classroom revolves around building confidence, resilience and self-esteem. Hart and Green (2014) show the link between self-esteem and achievement but remind us that young people's positive self-image and esteem can be challenged and may require 'maintenance' or support: 'anyone may be exposed to adversity at any point in their lives and may not cope with it successfully' (p. 4).

To address this, teachers need to think about how they develop mastery-oriented children who tend to: not see themselves as failing, engage in self-motivating strategies, engage in self-instruction or self-monitoring, remain confident that they would succeed, have an attitude that they could learn from their failures and do not see failure as a criticism of themselves as people (Dweck, 2000). The characteristics of the mastery-oriented child are illustrated in Figure 6.

Teachers would undoubtedly agree that this is the type of learner they would like to develop in their classroom. In practice this means:

- creating a positive learning environment
- developing good pedagogical practice
- working collaboratively.

Teacher–pupil interaction is important in the development of mastery-oriented children. The way you scaffold their learning, through the general techniques of questioning, prompting, praising, confirming, pointing things out to children and

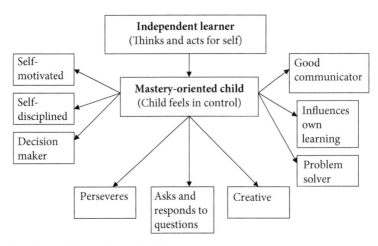

Fig. 6 Qualities of an independent learner

modelling, all have an impact on the development of positive dispositions in the child. Also, as has been discussed earlier in the book, good formative assessment, employing the techniques of assessment for learning, helps the child to develop independence in their learning. The following section considers some of the practical aspects of these approaches.

Teachers: what to do in practice

Some techniques for developing mastery-oriented children are:

- Children need the stimulation teachers give them and engage best when they have a 'can do' feeling.
- One central feature of making learning fun is that children are more likely to want to engage with it.
- Children are more likely to develop the habit of self-discipline if they feel empowered to approach whatever task they are given and feel that there is some chance of personal success.
- Areas that may be perceived as 'difficult' by some children provide an opportunity for teachers to 'break down' the learning process. Children should be taught how to approach a problem step by step, which brings greater focus to their thought process and their sense of achievement. Each step provides a small opportunity for success. With personal effort, determination and perseverance, everyone can achieve their potential.

Constructive marking and feedback are powerful tools for enabling children to take co-ownership of their work and move towards self-motivated learning and improvement. This has three core elements:

1. The child is fully aware of their learning objectives.
2. The child is made aware of the extent to which the learning objectives have been achieved.
3. The child knows how to go about achieving the shortfall in the learning objectives.

Teachers will probably give feedback both orally and through written comment, with oral feedback providing greater opportunity for a child's self-assessment. Written comments can be time-consuming for the teacher and careful thought needs to be given to the purpose of this feedback. Teacher feedback is only constructive when children are empowered and enabled to act upon it. Shirley Clarke (1998, p. 70), suggests that effective feedback in the primary classroom needs:

- to be based on clear learning intentions
- to take account of pupil self-evaluation
- to highlight where success occurred and where improvement could take place
- to be in a form which is accessible to the learner
- to give strategies for improvement
- allocated time in which to take place or be read
- some focused improvement, based on the feedback to take place.

Suitable teaching approaches (quality teaching and learning)

We know that high-quality teaching is the biggest single factor in the achievement of children and young people; this is particularly crucial for those from less advantaged families (Sutton Trust, 2011).

In practice these are borne out differently in the classroom and across the school; the synergy between the elements is a key consideration. Teacher beliefs – the reasons why you adopt particular practices and theories about learning – can be a central area for reflection. For example, by changing your level of aspiration for pupils you can adapt your established beliefs and behaviours; this can result in pupils with higher aspirations and better outcomes. Encouraging teachers to develop themselves, deepening their subject knowledge and learning to use it as effectively as possible, is self-evident. What can be lacking is a focus on the synergy between the other elements of quality teaching (Coe et. al., 2014) and the extent to which you as a teacher 'take ownership' for change. This section will consider key approaches for focusing on aspiration and access, leading to higher achievement.

Teachers: what to do in practice

Talking to children about what they know

Learning is a two-way process, where learners are involved in self-assessment and made aware of how and why they are learning. This concept of learning is also supported by Overall and Sangster (2006, p. 66). They refer to the centrality of the 'internal dialogue', which they define as 'talking within the head' – in the learning process. They propose paired or small group work as a natural means of enabling children to become aware of the 'how' and 'why' of learning. They further suggest that the interaction of the teacher with the learner in explaining how to carry out a particular task or getting them to talk 'about what they know' or how they know if they have completed a task 'well or badly' provides a natural means of enabling the child to become aware of the learning process. In addition, it provides a means of integrating children's self-assessment into practice. There is also much to be gained by thinking out aloud and planning this with the children in your class.

Harrison and Howard (2009, pp. 8–16) offer some practical suggestions for engaging children in talking about their learning.

1. Teachers valuing talk and dialogue with young children. Whilst young children may not share what might be called the 'language of learning' used by adults, when practitioners value young people's talk and engage in dialogue, the young people can 'both reveal their current thoughts and, by responding to others, begin to construct new ways of thinking about a topic or a skill'.
2. Teachers examining and developing their questioning strategies. 'Rich questions' provide opportunities for children to engage in thinking and debate. This has been described as using 'fat questions' that require answers of five words or more, as opposed to 'skinny questions' that generally require only a few or a single word to answer.
3. Teachers encouraging children to respond. All teachers should give children time to respond to questions. However, even marginal increases in the time allocated to waiting for a child's response can have maximal impacts. This can include developing a classroom environment where children feel free to discuss their ideas with their peers and teachers.
4. Teachers responding to or using pupils' contributions. Creating a climate where probing questions and discussion are integral to learning is not easy. However, teachers can ensure that their comments, body language and expressions are non-judgemental and that their interventions do

not 'cut-off' children's attempts to construct meaning and compare their ideas with their peers.

(Source: adapted from Harrison and Howard, 2009, pp. 8–16)

Providing children with the opportunity to discuss their work provides a means of effectivity re-channelling their thinking. Black and Wiliam (1998) highlighted the benefits for children, in terms of improved knowledge and understanding, when they have the opportunity to discuss their work with teachers. This can be done both formally and informally; often, this will be questioning children about their work. The following has been adapted from Black and Wiliam (1998, pp. 11–12) and provides a good framework for considering how to use questioning effectively:

- Give children *time to respond to questions*: **reflection time.**
- Let children *discuss their thinking in pairs* before one of the 'pair' reports back: **discussion time.**
- Give children a choice of answers and let them *vote* on the correct response: **consideration time.**
- *Good questions are hard to generate and practitioners should collaborate, and draw critically on outside sources, to collect such questions*: **development time** – it is good to write possible ways of both asking children questions and answering children's questions into short-term plans.

Good questioning is founded on the idea of teaching for independent learning. Teacher questions should challenge and encourage children in their learning and wider development. Questioning should provide opportunity for the children to start taking responsibility for their own learning, opening channels for thinking, creativity, problem-solving and decision-making. Black and Wiliam (1998, p. 11), in their study of assessment, highlighted examples of teachers (unconsciously) responding to children's questions in a way that prevents them moving forward in their learning. 'What the examples have in common', they state, 'is that the practitioner is looking for a particular response and lacks the flexibility or the confidence to deal with the unexpected.'

Teacher responses need to be constructive. They should motivate children, encourage them and move them towards self-mastery of skills and knowledge. It is important to remember that children's confidence develops progressively step by step and is powered by their successes – recall the adage of 'success breeds success'. This goal is best achieved by focusing on the individual child: their achievements and their continuing progress. By focusing on the child, teachers also provide opportunities for the child to self-assess. Whilst responses need to have a corrective aspect, failure should not be the focus of feedback; nor should teachers compare a child's achievement with that of their peers. Motivational feedback (which focuses on progress and success) is closely linked to enabling and equipping children to be ready, willing and able to learn in primary school settings and in their ongoing education.

Involving children in planning their next steps

The last few years have witnessed a shift in classroom and setting practice, particularly in the way in which children have become more involved in their own learning. There is the expectation that by making children fully aware of the learning objectives and outcomes of a particular activity/lesson and involving them in planning their next steps, teachers will enhance their learning. In practice how can this be achieved? Clarke (2002) suggests 'balancing the curriculum' to cover both the teaching of skills, concepts and knowledge and their application, and that 'sharing unit coverage throughout lessons and separating learning objectives from the context of learning' will help children to be more aware of the goals on which they need to focus and develop. Every child is unique and the extent to which that child has achieved the expected outcomes will determine the next steps in his/her learning.

Essentially, involving children in the planning of their learning helps children to take ownership of their progress and achievements. This will involve teachers guiding children in their decision-making; but this is guided choice, and not necessarily free choice. Child-initiated activities will lend themselves more easily to this type of child involvement than adult-led activities. However, there are always opportunities to involve children in discussing 'what comes next?'

The responsibility is with the practitioner to consider how 'next steps' can be effectively implemented (for example, through constructive questioning or inclusive dialogue). For child-initiated activities, allowing time for the children to plan and discuss their activity in advance will bring greater clarity to the children's thought processes and will provide further opportunity for stimulating ideas. There will be children who do not want to plan – these children should be supported and encouraged to get on with the task in hand. The High/Scope curriculum is founded on this type of activity and is useful for developing children's independence.

Differentiated teaching to meet individual needs and appropriate interventions

Differentiation is about providing different pupils with different learning paths to enable them to get the best possible outcomes. It can encompass adaptation of the curriculum, using different processes to ensure learning has taken place, a focus on pupil output and/or a consideration of the learning environment. A key feature in primary schools that get good outcomes for their pupils is the way teachers plan together; they identify perceived 'difficult' areas in the curriculum and consider effective ways of addressing it. The introduction in England of the South Asian mastery approach to teaching maths has seen a move away from differentiated content to differentiated processes, where all children are provided with the same maths-rich experiences and children who failed to grasp a concept in the previous lesson spend a short time with a teacher before the next lesson to go over it.

Creating the right learning environment in helping all children to develop the necessary skills, attributes and emotional integrity to become independent learners is very important for practice. Whitebread et al. (2005) suggest, amongst other characteristics, that it is associated with self-regulation, taking 'ownership' for learning and understanding the 'how' of learning.

Teachers: what to do in practice

In practice, Williams (2003, p. 130) suggests that teaching for independent learning means adapting the provision to give 'children the chance to make choices, organise themselves and respond with energy and enthusiasm'. What is clear, from both Williams' delineation of independent learning and the idea of independent learning within a social-cognitive construct, is that in practice it involves a particular approach to learning and development that should be integrated into day-to-day practice.

Teachers need to nurture an environment where all children share in decisions relating to their learning and learning environment. The art of decision-making is encouraged by allowing children to put forward their opinion in an environment where they know their opinion matters. It is vital to develop a strong framework for practice, within which children can become competent and confident learners. Asking children for their opinion gives them the feeling of being in control, of shared responsibility and of owning their learning.

Williams (2003, p. 71) highlights the benefits of 'a learning environment which promotes independence' in terms of providing 'a framework for children's developing self-esteem and responsibility'. By involving children in the development of the physical learning environment, the practitioner will have enabled them to exercise choice and initiated some of the thinking skills needed for solving problems. For example:

- Which resources to use and why?
- Where to find the resources and why?
- How to use the resources.

However, working through an activity or problem until the end is vital if children are to learn how to persevere, particularly in difficult situations. Repeatedly allowing children to *plan, do* and *review* their activities provides many opportunities to weigh up the pros and cons of making an error of judgment. If, for example, within a short period of time after embarking on an activity, a child realises that he/she has chosen the wrong resource for the desired outcome then the reselection of a more appropriate resource should be considered. But what happens if the resource a child has selected will give the desired outcome, but a different resource would have been better? These are the types of issues that should be discussed with the children. What is their view? For the teacher, it is a matter of altering children's perceptions of decision-making; an error of judgement, for example, in the choice of resource is not a failure. Supported in this way, children will independently change an inappropriate resource and happily continue their activity.

Learning the 'art' of perseverance hinges on following through plans and ownership of learning; children should be encouraged to complete tasks. The following framework for planning, developed by Williams (2003, p. 19) from research findings in 80 primary schools, provides a valuable framework for enabling children to develop the inner integrity to persevere in learning:

- Children should plan some of their own activities and have some say in the order in which they do the tasks.
- Let children plan out step-by-step actions to carry out their own activity.
- Support children in developing their own action plans.
- Use charts or diagrams for children to refer to when trying to solve particular problems.
- Children should always have the opportunity to contribute their own ideas and to act independently with all tasks.

Appropriate interventions

For some children interventions may better support their learning and development. These can be put in place as appropriate. They should be regularly monitored in the context of the child's progress. If the child is not making expected progress with a particular intervention, practitioners should consider what else may be needed. It may mean changing the intervention or it may mean moving towards a formal needs assessment for children identified as having a SEN – the next step in the EHC Plan process.

Teachers: what to do in practice

If a child is not making expected progress, you need to add extra tasks to your planning for the child, implement these and closely monitor the child's progress. If after a certain (short) period of time (this should be set in advance) the child is still not making the expected progress, interventions can be put in place. How you do this can depend on the school's policy, or what you think may work for the child.

Examples include maths or literacy interventions, where a child can work with a teaching assistant in the classroom, or it may involve a group of children. This should be discussed with teaching assistants, so that they know how to implement and develop the intervention, how to monitor the child, what progress and learning looks like in practice, how to question and prompt children to move them forward in their learning and the importance of an aspirational outlook for children's learning and achievements.

Teachers need to make time before and after the intervention lesson to discuss the children's progress with the teaching assistant. It can also be helpful to support parents and carers in developing the relevant activity at home. For example, parents and carers could be shown how to use a particular resource at home and how to work with their child on the tasks. The important issue with interventions is to use them if you believe they will help the child to make progress; but the focus in class should be on high-quality teaching and an inclusive approach, with appropriate differentiation of tasks.

Conclusion

This chapter has explored approaches, practices and techniques for raising aspirations (teachers, pupils, parents and carers, leaders and other staff) and removing barriers to learning, leading to increased achievement for all pupils.

In summary, it has shown that when teachers are given responsibility for all children in their class it is possible to improve children's outcomes by:

- taking an active role in the assessment and monitoring of pupils
- being more frequently involved in reviewing individual pupil targets (and with parents and carers)
- data-led discussions with other colleagues and/or the senior leadership team
- planning with other teachers for differentiation
- engaging parents in their child's learning
- increased teacher knowledge and understanding of pupils, resulting in a more personalised approach to teaching and learning within the classroom.

Chapter 4 takeaway

Teaching tip

It is a good idea at the outset to know the characteristics of the various independent learning skills discussed in the chapter. Complete the following table. It will support you in reflecting on how you integrate the necessary skills for independent learning into daily practice and/or how you could do it better.

Independent learning skill	Characteristics	How can this be developed in practice?
Self-motivation		
Self-discipline		
Decision-making		
Perseverance		
Creativity		
Asks and responds to questions		
Problem-solving		
Influences own learning		
Good communicator		

Pass it on

Organise a number of 'planning for differentiation' sessions with your colleagues. For each area of the curriculum consider where the perceived 'difficult' areas might lie and how they can be effectively addressed in practice for *all* children.

Share and tweet

Tweet, using the hashtag #BloomsCPD: moving children closer to independent thought and action is the hallmark of a great teacher.

CPD book club recommendation

Inside The Black Box: Raising Standards Through Classroom Assessment by Paul Black and Dylan Wiliam

(See bibliography)

This book is relatively short and precise and easy to use as a result. It will help you to think about formative assessment and how to develop it more effectively in the classroom.

Love to Teach: Bring Out the Best in You and Your Class by Sonia Blandford

(See bibliography)

This book considers raising attainment in the context of some of the challenges teachers face in the classroom. Its focus is on meeting these challenges in a way that enhances teacher wellbeing and job satisfaction.

Bloggers' corner

Look up the blogs at the Institute of Education, UCL.
Available at: http://www.ucl.ac.uk/ioe/news-events/ioe-experts-blog

TO DO LIST:

❑ Having read this chapter, reflect on how you can better build the core in children in the classroom (aspiration: *I can*; access: *I do*; attainment: *I have*; and achievement: *I am*).

❑ Discuss with colleagues how you could further develop this (e.g. form a network group, through focused CPD, etc.).

❑ To what extent do your classroom practices and pedagogy support and encourage children to become independent learners (thinking and acting for themselves)?

❑ Read *Inside the Black Box* and *Love to Teach*.

❑ Look up and read some of the IoE, UCL blogs.

5 Putting it into practice

This chapter further develops the key strategies for building the core in children (aspiration, access, attainment and achievement) through a series of case studies. The case studies focus on the key strategies discussed in Chapter 4. Each case study is followed by suggested actions for implementing it in your classroom or school and a reflection for you to consider your current practice in this area and how you could do it better.

The chapter finishes with a series of self-reflection questions for you to focus the learning in this chapter and further develop your own practice.

Engaging parents and carers

Case study 1: Thorney Close Primary, Sunderland

Context

Thorney Close primary school has 271 pupils on roll, with a higher than average proportion of pupils on SEN Support (18 per cent) and also those eligible for Free School Meals (FSM) (32 per cent). It was rated good at its last Ofsted inspection in 2013.

Two target groups of 11 pupils were identified within Key Stage 1 and Key Stage 2; of these pupils, 73 per cent were entitled to Pupil Premium and 32 per cent were on SEN Support. They were identified as pupils who would benefit from greater parent engagement in their learning and from supporting that both in school and at home.

The school already worked hard to get parents to attend events such as summer parties or school productions, but when the focus was on learning, they were less successful. A core of parents did not turn up for parents' evenings.

Approach

The school introduced structured conversations through their work with Achievement for All. The school focused the meetings on how well the child was doing and what the parents' hopes were for their children. They identified a need for greater flexibility in offering times for appointments. A personal invitation from the class teacher was followed by a phone call(s), and catching them in the playground, to arrange an appointment that would suit the family. In one case a teacher made five different appointments with the parents, but eventually succeeded in meeting with them. The longer meeting time of at least 20 minutes meant that parents and carers felt their viewpoint was valued.

It became clear that children needed more support to understand what they had to do to move forward in their learning. Parents and carers were involved in short-term targets, and the school developed a visual tool using RAG ratings to demonstrate measures such as attendance, punctuality and progress by subject to show how much progress their child was making. Although parents and carers valued their child's happiness and confidence, academic attainment was a low priority. The SLT decided to raise the profile of attainment and launched the 'We Are Proud' celebration.

Using iPads, teachers captured the successes of each child, what they could do now that they couldn't do before, from reading to running, and brought it together as a film. The children worked together to design a personal invitation to every parent, and other family members were encouraged to attend. Parents received a text, a phone call and a mention on the Thorney Close App (designed by the school as a communication tool via mobile technology) and the school newsletter: *The Thorney Times*. The film was shown with popcorn and drinks, and parents, teachers and children talked together about their progress.

Impact

Parental engagement increased from 58 per cent to 92 per cent across three terms for the Key Stage 1 group and from 64 per cent to 100 per cent for the Key Stage 2 group; over 90 per cent of parents and carers attended the We Are Proud celebration. The children are growing in confidence and some of the initiatives are used with other pupils across the school. Many teachers have adopted the 'celebration' initiative capturing successes in photos on the walls of the classrooms and in home–school reports.

(Source: Achievement for All)

Implementing it in your classroom/school

- Be flexible in meeting times for parents and carers. It is vital to work with them to agree times.

- Parents and carers need help in understanding education terminology; present information in a format they can engage with.
- Develop and build on successful ways to communicate with parents and carers in a way with which you are also familiar.
- Take time to reflect on improved practice and celebrate it with the school community.

Reflect on practice

- How do you currently engage/involve parents and carers in their child's learning?
- How could you better engage parents and carers in their child's learning?

Tracking and measuring progress in maths

Case study 2: Victoria Lane Academy, Coundon, Durham

Context

Victoria Lane Academy, on the edge of a rural village in County Durham, is situated in one of the ten per cent most deprived neighbourhoods in England. In July 2011, it was one of the lowest performing primary schools in Durham. A forced takeover in 2013 brought the school into a multi-academy trust of seven schools. Today Victoria Lane Academy is rated good by Ofsted and pupil performance in maths is above the national average. There are 171 pupils on roll (three to 11 years); 20 per cent of pupils are on SEN Support and 34 per cent of pupils are eligible for free school meals.

The headteacher started in September 2013 and made a number of immediate changes, including introducing the 'new' draft maths curriculum to give all teachers 'a head start'. Life without levels in the same year saw the development of the school's own assessment system, based on key objectives for the year group. From this base the school developed a cohort action plan for all pupils, supported by the rigorous analysis of pupil data every half term. This approach meant all teachers were part of and contributing to the change process from the outset.

Approach

Assessment and planning

Two weeks before pupils are taught a new topic in maths, each child does a written pre-assessment to find out where they are in their learning. Teachers plan for each child, differentiating work accordingly. Planning is on a daily basis; after day one of teaching the topic, teachers plan for day two. At the end of the topic, which usually lasts two weeks, children have a post-assessment. It is very positive for children's learning; a teacher can say 'this is where you were two weeks ago and look where you are now'. This type of approach enables teachers to quickly identify any child who needs support.

To provide greater evidence of learning, the school introduced maths stickers, which include extension tasks and further challenges at the end of lessons.

The approach to maths is based on 'real-life' scenarios. For example, brochures and catalogues are used and children work out the price of a holiday or they may use menus to work out the price of meals. One year group is studying America and is looking at the different metrics used. Games through ICT, and in particular Mathletics, are used across the school. The annual business project, where children make a product to sell – for example, cakes – provides children with the opportunity to cost materials and work out profit margins; each child is given £5 at the outset. Children are often surprised by the profit they make.

There is a big focus across the school on number, and in addition to maths lessons, every class has maths and maths skills on a daily basis. Resources include those from NRICH, and the NCETM maths guide is used by teachers.

The development of maths skills is applied across the curriculum. This was initiated through an evaluation and consideration of opportunities for maths across all subjects, enabling teachers to identify less obvious areas where maths could be introduced; the headteacher believes the new curriculum provides more opportunities than before.

Children at Victoria Lane Academy love maths. Many don't read well, but maths 'clicks' with them and parents value maths. This gives the children confidence. The particular approach leads to accelerated progress in maths; the headteacher attributes this to the school's pre-teaching rather than catch-up approach. For example, in Year 3 (where pre-teaching has been trialled), a teacher will identify an area where a pupil needs some teaching before the lesson; this pupil or small group of pupils will have a short session at lunchtime with the teacher.

Pupil groupings and feedback
There is a teaching assistant in every class; they are deployed according to their strengths. A TA strong in maths will go into maths classes, whilst those stronger in literacy will go into literacy classes. All TAs have appropriate training and give verbal feedback to children during the lesson.

Immediate feedback to children is of central importance in the school's approach to maths. As the headteacher says, 'children's misconceptions can be addressed straight away – otherwise it may be too late'.

Children are grouped according to their pre-assessment; a child good at numbers will work with children of similar ability in this area, but the same child may be less gifted at shapes, so will work with similar-ability children on shapes.

Boosters
There are maths skills after-school booster clubs for children in Years 2 and 6; the focus is on applying skills. Pupil Premium funding was used to buy in a specialist teacher for the booster club in Year 6, which also includes developing the skills of children working at/towards Level 6. Year 2 booster club is one night a week.

Interventions
Interventions are used when they are needed for some pupils. The school invested in Numicon, again using Pupil Premium funding for the resources. The maths co-ordinator was trained in the approach and shared this with all teachers across the school. Numicon is used for number development in the foundation stage and Key Stage 1 and as an intervention, for any child who needs it, in Key Stage 2.

Impact: key to success
- Pre- and post-assessment of children for new topic.
- Ongoing daily planning of class teachers.
- Setting maths within a meaningful 'real-life' context.
- Engaging children in 'real-life' problem-solving.

(Source: Knowles, 2017, 'Closing the attainment gap in maths: a study of good practice in early years and primary settings', Fair Education Alliance)

Implementing it in your classroom/school

- Develop an action plan for each pupil, focusing on data analysis.
- Plan for the topic in advance (this is best done as a group of teachers).
- Develop a pre-test for each topic (you can initially select one subject – maths) to identify each pupil's knowledge and understanding.
- Adapt the topic accordingly.
- Assess pupil learning daily – during and after they have been taught the topic.
- Consider what you need to change for pupils who have failed to grasp a concept.
- Develop a post-test.
- Celebrate pupil success after the topic.

Reflect on practice

- How effective is your current analysis of pupil data?
- Do you analyse data often enough?
- How could you better track pupil progress and understanding?

A focus on SEND, differentiation and interventions

Case study 3: The Beeches Primary School, Peterborough

Context

The Beeches, a larger than average-sized primary school, has 630 pupils on roll. A community school, The Beeches is situated in Peterborough. Many pupils join the school part way through their primary education, often from abroad and speaking no English; the vast majority of pupils are EAL (94 per cent). The proportion of pupils eligible and claiming free school meals is above average at 17 per cent, as is the proportion of children with special educational needs and/or disabilities (SEND); 28 per cent of pupils are SEN Support. At its last Ofsted inspection (March 2014), the school was rated good.

Approach

The school highlighted interventions and the role of the class teacher and teaching assistants as areas for development. The school recognised that children with SEND in Year 2 were spending large portions of the day being taught outside the classroom in intervention groups led by a higher-level teaching assistant (HLTA). Through analysis of the data it was clear that whilst children with SEND in most year groups were making good or better progress, this Year 2 group of children were making less than expected progress. An internal review by the school and an educational psychologist showed that teachers needed to have ownership of the progress and wellbeing for these pupils.

Consequently, the focus across the school became quality first teaching, differentiation and support within the classroom. Teachers, the SENCO and a designated member of the SLT met on a regular basis throughout the year to review what was working well and to make further, smaller changes as required – a process that became increasingly positive.

Impact

The target pupils in Year 2 made outstanding progress; this approach has now been implemented with underachieving pupils across the school. The profile of lower-attaining children is regularly discussed in staff meetings and by the SLT. Teachers have taken responsibility for tracking the progress of all pupils identified as SEN; generally, across the school, analysis and use of data has improved. As a result of improvement in the quality of teaching, and interventions such as Forest Schools, Children's University and the employment of a family support worker, pupils have become more engaged in lessons and have increasing levels of self-esteem. Parent and carer engagement has improved significantly.

(Source: Achievement for All)

Implementing it in your classroom/school

- Make regular and effective use of your own and the school's data-tracking system, particularly for children in the lower attainment cohort or those at risk of underachievement.
- Plan for differentiation for lower-attaining pupils in an integrated class setting; this could be by content.
- Involve your teaching assistant(s) in this process.

- Ensure your TAs know and understand the aims of your lessons and their role in pupil progress and attainment.
- Take time before and after a lesson to discuss individual/identified children's learning during the lesson with the TAs.
- Show the children you value the TAs.
- Ensure quality first teaching is in place before you consider an intervention for a pupil (could this pupil be supported through 1:1 in the classroom or pre-teaching before a lesson, etc.?).

Reflect on practice

- Do you closely monitor and evaluate any interventions you have put in place?
- How could you better support children with SEND or those at risk of underachievement/underachieving in the whole-class setting?

Quality first teaching is fundamental to ensuring all children make progress

Case study 4: Brightlingsea Infants, Essex

Context

Brightlingsea is a three-form entry primary school in the coastal Essex town of Brightlingsea. There is an increasing population of residents moving to the area from London and other towns, with the result that there are 338 pupils on roll. The proportion of pupils claiming free school meals is around the national average at 14 per cent. Pupils identified as SEN Support is below the national average of 11.6 per cent at 4.7 per cent; those with a Statement or EHC Plan is 0.6 per cent. At its last Ofsted inspection (May 2013), the school was rated outstanding. Prior to making changes within the school, classroom culture and practice was patchy, the impact of interventions was unclear and there were variable expectations of children.

Approach

The focus in the school is on quality first teaching. Teachers take full responsibility for all children in their class – they prepare for structured conversations and regular pupil progress meetings. Teachers review their routine practice in the classroom and are encouraged to consider whether all children can access the same quality of teaching. All teaching staff and teaching assistants are trained in Fischer Family Trust Wave 3. Teachers ensure that every child has access to quality teaching; interventions are only used when children fail to make expected progress.

As the headteacher said: 'What we try to do is look at what changes we can make to quality first teaching before going in with an intervention – which can be costly and only impact on one child. A change of practice can impact on many and improve quality overall.'

TAs have been trained in narrative therapy, with groups of staff trained in specialist interventions such as Gym Trail; a number of staff have been trained as play leaders to help improve behaviour at lunchtime and playtimes. The senior leadership team also considered common practice across the school to ensure children can access learning quickly – this includes all classrooms being set out in the same way so children are familiar and comfortable with the environment when they change class.

Impact

Over the past year Brightlingsea has focused on embedding key practice. Teachers have full ownership and accountability for the progress of all children in their classes. They set targets, monitor pupil learning and assessment and have regular pupil progress meetings, ensuring a continuing focus; teacher expectations for pupil progress have increased. Structured conversations, sometimes in adapted form, are now run with all parents, who get at least three 20-minute consultations each year. Children are only added to the SEN register if there is genuine cause to do so and not because they are not making expected progress.

(Source: Achievement for All)

Implementing it in your classroom/school

- For each child consider whether there is one extra thing they need to be able to access this piece of learning (e.g. a resource, a few words of encouragement, input from a TA, glasses – is the child's eyesight good? etc.).
- Work effectively with your TA – take time before and after to discuss children's learning and progress – what are your expectations for the children's learning?
- Ensure the learning environment supports engagement with learning.

- If TAs take intervention groups, ensure they know and understand the curriculum area, know the aims and expectation for each child's learning, record attainment and test learning after the lesson.
- Monitor the progress and learning of any child involved in an intervention on a weekly basis.
- If the intervention is not working, stop it or change it.

Reflect on practice

- Do you ensure every child has an opportunity to contribute to the class?
- How could you do this better?

A whole-school approach to maths using the mastery approach

Case study 5: Parkfield Primary School, Birmingham (an academy converter since 2013)

Context

Parkfield, situated in one of the ten per cent most deprived neighbourhoods in the country, converted to an academy in 2013. In 2015, the school was awarded a National Pupil Premium Award for being one of the most improved schools in the country in terms of the attainment and progress of disadvantaged pupils since 2011. At its most recent inspection in 2017, it was rated outstanding by Ofsted. There are 738 pupils on roll, of whom 93 per cent are EAL and 27 per cent are eligible for FSM; just five per cent of pupils are identified as SEN Support.

In 2013, the assistant head became the maths lead for the school and made a number of changes in both primary and early years: 'to address maths in primary school, you need to start in the early years'. Through her own training, research and experience, she realised that teachers need focused, maths-specific CPD in order to enhance the learning experiences of pupils – particularly with the higher expectations of the National Curriculum and statutory assessments.

Approach

When the assistant head became maths lead across the school, she began by completely raising the profile of maths. The phrase 'I can't do maths' was banned and there was a focus on making maths enjoyable for everyone – staff, children and parents. The school is a strategic partner with Central Maths Hub and the maths lead is a Mastery Specialist teacher and joint Mastery Lead for the Central Hub. The focus in maths is the mastery approach – teaching children to understand concepts through a concrete, pictorial and abstract approach.

A programme of intensive training was introduced for all staff in 2013/2014; one after-school session per month, with a particular focus on teacher subject knowledge. This has now switched to a rolling programme of more bespoke CPD for staff who identify gaps in their knowledge or for NQTs, student teachers or any teacher new to the school. The maths lead and senior leaders closely monitor flipcharts used for lessons, which have replaced paper plans at this school, and regularly check children's learning in books.

The school was involved in trialling the Singapore textbooks and has since been gradually introducing Maths No Problem books. They are now used in Years 1–4; teachers use the textbooks to support planning. The maths lead sees the textbooks as a 'tool'; they have helped teachers to adapt to the mastery approach of teaching. She is quick to add that 'It's not what you do, but the way that you do it. It is the pedagogy which can transform teaching; the textbooks are a just good resource, not a magic wand.'

The school is well resourced in maths from the nursery to Year 6. Staff are well trained to know which resource to use for which mathematical concept. Resources are carefully planned into activities to get the most out of them; use of resources is not haphazard.

All children work in mixed ability groups; this is influenced by the maths policy of not deciding in advance that a child 'cannot do' maths. Children's learning is scaffolded and the rate at which children work is not necessarily accelerated; they tend to work at the same pace, but some will work at greater depth than others.

There is a very secure assessment system in place. Years 1–4 have split maths lessons. That is, they have half the lesson, a break and come back for the second half of the lesson. Years 5 and 6 have an hour of maths, whilst early years children have 20 minutes (in early years, maths is mainly developed through play). In this way children are closely monitored and if a child fails to grasp the concept, they have 20 minutes (1:1 or a small group of children) with a teacher on the same day.

Interventions

Every Child Counts programmes were introduced a few years ago; the programmes were very successful. However, since the school changed their approach to maths, gaps in children's learning are identified more quickly. The resources and some of the strategies of Every Child Counts are still used across the school, and what they learnt through the intervention programmes has supported their implementation and development of the mastery approach. There is still a need for ongoing intervention, and with older children Numbers Count, Success at Arithmetic and 1st Class @ Number are used for identified children.

Cross-curricular

The maths lead believes that the maths curriculum has changed so much that there would not be enough time to cover everything in one hour of maths alone; it needs to come into other subjects. Ideas might include children using stop watches in PE to time themselves running and then recording this graphically or in a table. Equally in science, there are many opportunities for measuring and recording findings in a graph or table. A lot of teaching is in topics across the school; a recent topic on the Ancient Greeks enabled the children to look at the various aspects of geometry. Through making such cross-curricular links, children also see the importance of maths and the wider applications it has, beyond just number.

Parent engagement/home learning

Bespoke maths workshops are organised for parents at least once a term. They are based on 'home' maths – that is, parents doing maths with their children and not teaching 'new' maths. They focus on maths as fun and include games parents can do with their child for five minutes in the evening. These workshops address areas such as counting, numbers, number bonds and the vocabulary around maths. The aim is to enable parents to be interested, enthusiastic and happy about maths and doing maths with their children. Mathletics is available for Years 2–6, where the children can log on and do this at home; parent workshops teach parents how to monitor this work at home.

Impact: key to success

- Good development of teacher subject knowledge, built up through ongoing and focused CPD.
- Children starting lessons with a problem written on the board and practical apparatus to explore this problem.

- Teacher research.
- The learning from being involved with the Shanghai teacher exchange, Singapore-style textbooks and NCETM mastery programme.
- Enabling everyone to enjoy maths and be happy doing maths.

(Source: Knowles, 2017, 'Closing the attainment gap in maths: a study of good practice in early years and primary settings', Fair Education Alliance)

Implementing it in your classroom/school

- Develop your knowledge on maths and maths teaching and learning (where are the gaps?).
- Plan with other teachers, including how you will address perceived difficult areas with children to improve children's understanding.
- Develop a whole-class mixed ability approach, giving all children the same maths-rich experience.
- Have sameday 20-minute keep-up sessions for children who do not grasp a concept.
- Focus on metacognition with children.
- Focus on numbers, reasoning and problem-solving.
- Play games in maths to develop resilience.
- Involve parents and carers in their children's learning of maths.

Reflect on practice

- Do you have a whole-school approach to maths in your classroom? (Equally this works well with literacy.)
- How could you better develop it?

Self-reflection questions

The following are a series of self-reflection questions. They cover the issues addressed by the case studies and further questions relating to the wider context of raising attainment. The aim is help you reflect on what you have read in the book up to this point and to take your learning a step further.

Working with parents and carers

- Do you involve parents and carers in children's learning?
- Do you meet parents and carers individually to discuss their child's interests and learning?
- Do you discuss and decide children's learning targets with their parents and carers?
- Do you ensure that parents and carers know how to use resources and equipment that is sent home?
- Do you have workshops for parents and carers to support the development of literacy and numeracy and other subjects in the home environment?
- Do you encourage parents and carers to do 'five minutes' a day of fun maths and literacy activities with their children at home?

The physical environment

- Do you have interactive learning activities on the wall appropriate for all children?
- Do you have resources clearly labelled and sorted and appropriately adapted for children with SEND, low- and high-achieving children and children whose first language is not English?
- Do you, your teaching assistants and all the children know how to use each resource?
- Are children allowed to select their own resources?
- Are children allowed to move resources freely around the classroom?
- Do you have activity corners? (e.g. reading, maths, science, geography)
- Do you have a learning activity on each child's desk when they arrive in school? (e.g. a piece of maths equipment or a word search)
- Do you involve children in planning the learning environment?

Planning

- Does your planning start from where the children are in their learning?
- Do you apply aspiration, access and achievement to each child in your planning?
- Do you consider individual barriers to learning and consider what one thing could be put in place for this child to be able to access this activity?
- Do you plan for the majority of children and have more individualised activities for higher/lower or middle-achieving children?
- Does the National Curriculum provide your framework for planning?
- Does your long-term plan inform your medium-term plan, which in turn informs your short-term plan?
- Do parent and carer views on their child's learning feed into your planning?

- Do you do planning with colleagues?
- Do you plan with other teachers for differentiation?
- Does one teacher write up the plans for all after discussion?
- Does your planning focus on perceived difficult areas of learning for children and how you will address this?
- Do you have a bank of appropriate prompt questions for children that are aspirational and support children's independence in learning?
- Do you tailor activities to the individual needs of the child?
- Do you discuss activities/assessment and expectations with teaching assistants prior to lessons?
- Do you follow up with teaching assistants after the lessons?

Your Pupil Premium provision

- Do your Pupil Premium students have the same learning opportunities as other children?
- Are they able to access the learning opportunities?
- Do you show them that you have high expectations for their learning and achievement?
- Do you provide 'keep up' one-to-one or small-group sessions for Pupil Premium children or others who have failed to grasp a concept in the lesson?
- Do you closely monitor their progress?
- Do you make changes quickly if they are not making expected progress?
- If you have a set of exercise books to mark, do you mark their work first?
- Do you actively think how you can support them in making accelerated progress?

Teaching all children

- Do you have good knowledge of each subject you teach?
- Is your subject knowledge developed in the context of children's learning?
- Do you have an array of different teaching techniques that you use frequently and regularly?
- Do you scaffold children's learning?

Working with teaching assistants

- Do you ensure that teaching assistants know the aim, purpose and expected outcomes of interventions they teach?

- Do you ensure they know their role in increasing pupil progress and attainment?
- Do you ensure they are aware of the need to develop their subject knowledge of the curriculum in which they are involved?
- Do your teaching assistants know how to question pupils to further develop their learning?
- Do you take time to plan with or talk to teaching assistants prior to a lesson?
- Do you put time aside to hear their feedback on pupils after a lesson/intervention?
- Do you include how you will effectively deploy/work with teaching assistants in your planning?

Planning for progress

- Do you identify clear teaching objectives and content?
- Do you set tasks that challenge and interest pupils? Do you have appropriate and demanding expectations?
- Do you set clear targets for pupils' learning, building on prior attainment?
- Do you effectively identify pupils' needs?
- Do you plan in opportunities for pupil personal, social and cultural development?

Making progress

- Do you let children know at the outset of a topic/lesson what they will be learning and why?
- Do you ask children to discuss problem-solving in pairs?
- Do you break learning down into small steps?
- Do you ask children to present findings/a topic in front of the class?
- Do you encourage and support children in developing a creative project (e.g. designing a new school play area/garden)?
- Do you ensure that praise is motivational and supports independence in learning (e.g. not using phrases like 'You're so good at English' or 'You're so intelligent')?
- Do you give encouraging feedback regularly (e.g. I know you can do it, etc.)?
- Do you ask children to recall one new thing they have learnt after each topic/lesson?

Assessment

- Does your assessment of pupils help them to know how to improve?
- Do you engage children in self-assessment?

- Does your assessment address how children learn?
- Is your assessment sensitive and constructive?
- Do you feed back there and then to pupils?
- Does feedback foster motivation?
- Does your assessment help the children to better understand the learning objectives?
- Do you celebrate success?
- Do you do pre- and post-assessment for a new topic, planning learning experiences accordingly?

Using data

- Do you make effective use of assessment data?
- Do you regularly review assessment data of Pupil Premium pupils, those with SEND and others vulnerable to underachievement?
- Do you have regular data-led discussions with other leaders of learning?
- Do you interrogate the data-making comparisons within the class, how pupils are performing against similar schools in the area and how your pupils are performing nationally?
- Do you regularly use the data to identify gaps in children's learning?

Provision for wider opportunities

- Do you provide extra-curricular clubs for children at lunchtime/after school (e.g. sports, drama, music, debating, science, maths or book club)?
- Have you carried out an audit of the extra-curricular activities you provide?
- Have you asked the children what clubs they would like (and possibly why)?
- Given that children with SEND are less likely to attend extra-curricular activities than other children, have you considered what extra activities all children would like?
- Have you considered how you will enable all children to access the extra-curricular activities they would like to attend?
- Have you encouraged and supported children in developing their own activities/clubs?
- Do you monitor children's attendance and enjoyment at extra-curricular activities?
- Do you take this a step further and monitor attendance and enjoyment against their progress/attainment?

Chapter 5 takeaway

Teaching tip

Reflect on each of the case studies and consider how you can further develop your practice in these areas. The following questions will help you to focus on key points from each case study:

- How could you initiate better parental engagement for children whose parents are not involved with the school or their child's learning?
- Do you have an effective pupil-tracking system in place?
- What criteria do you use for putting interventions into place?
- Do you regularly give children the opportunity to stand up in front of the class and talk about one of their interests or some aspect of learning?
- Do you discuss perceived difficult areas of learning and how you will teach them when you are planning with colleagues?

Pass it on

Organise a session with colleagues on a whole-class/school approach to raising attainment in maths or literacy.

Share and tweet

Tweet, using the hashtag #BloomsCPD: case studies give you focused approaches to improving practice.

CPD book club recommendation

Don't Like Mondays? by Sonia Blandford

(See bibliography)

This book gives teachers an insight into the ideas and thoughts of those children and young people who find school challenging. With personal stories and ideas from children and young people, it gives teachers ideas on how to make change in the classroom that will enable children to make progress and enjoy learning.

Knowles (2017) 'Closing the attainment gap in maths: a study of good practice in early years and primary settings', London: Fair Education Alliance

This case study report showcases a range of practical ideas to improve achievement in maths. The report shows that when primary schools and early years settings have a whole approach to maths, children's outcomes are better and in many cases above expectations. A whole-school approach means focusing on maths across leadership, attitudes, teaching and learning, progress and assessment, the environment, parent and carer engagement, wider opportunities and wellbeing.

Bloggers' corner

Look up more case studies for improving children's outcomes and closing the gap at Achievement for All. Available at: https://afaeducation.org/our-impact/impact-reports/impact-reports/

TO DO LIST:

☐ Having read this chapter, reflect on how you can better develop your practice in the areas covered by the case studies (where are your strengths and where are your development areas?).

☐ Discuss with colleagues how you could further develop this (e.g. form a network group, through focused CPD, etc.).

☐ To what extent are your classroom practices and pedagogy inclusive of all children?

☐ Read *Don't Like Mondays?* by Sonia Blandford.

☐ Look up and read some of the recommended case studies on the Achievement for All website.

6 Monitoring and evaluation

Effective monitoring and evaluation are central aspects of change. You will want to know if it is working and if not, why not and are things better than they were before the change was implemented? Monitoring is an ongoing process and can be thought of as tracking progress throughout the change. Everard et al. (2004) set monitoring within the context of 'yardsticks' by which to recognise when the objectives, at each stage, are being achieved, and which can be used 'to set a ratchet to prevent backsliding'. Evaluation, on the other hand, is an assessment of the outcomes and impact; it enables the teacher to compare the actual outcomes with the expected outcomes. Monitoring provides the basis for effective evaluation, where evaluation provides the evidence-based data. Reflecting on the definitions clearly underlines the centrality of well thought-through planning, with expected 'success criteria' in place for each stage of the change and 'back up' plans 'to take corrective action in case of a shortfall' (Everard et al., 2004, p. 285) if it is not working. This chapter looks at effective monitoring and evaluation in the context of changes you make to raise the attainment of all children in your classroom; it is about monitoring and evaluating your progress in improving classroom practice and self-development, along with evaluating and monitoring children's progress in light of the changes.

Monitoring

Monitoring is critical to the successful implementation of plans at any level of practice: strategic or operational. Effective monitoring enables teachers to obtain the best results from the available resources. The process of monitoring enables teachers, leaders and teams to work towards agreed objectives. Once objectives have been agreed the teacher can move forward with confidence. From clear objectives comes a sense of purpose. It may be difficult to set objectives clearly in place at the outset, but it is important to do so if the plan is to work effectively. Figure 7 illustrates the process of monitoring a plan's progress and is made easier

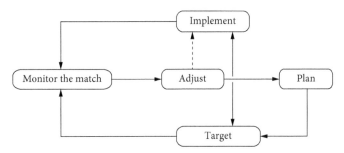

Fig. 7 Development planning feedback loop (Hargreaves, 1995)

if objectives are **clear** and **practical** and agreed by all members of a team (if working within a team).

Monitoring also provides the basis for evaluating practice, enabling teachers to measure and compare performance against agreed criteria and consider the strengths and weaknesses of continuing with the plan. Everard et al. (2004) advocate setting up, 'as part of the overall plan for change', some means of both 'gathering reliable information and analysing it... in order to measure if the change has been effective and has become truly assimilated'. They highlight the 'future scenario' description as a means of ascertaining the appropriate measures to employ. In addition, they suggest that the following techniques can be used as a means of measuring success, where the emphasis is on the 'actual outcomes of the change':

- 'A checklist of procedures
- A questionnaire about role responsibilities (if working as a team)
- An analysis of exam results or an attitude survey to be completed by those most likely to know if the change has been successful e.g. the pupils.'

(Source: Everard et al., 2004)

Monitoring will provide a framework in which teachers can reflect on their own practice, an outcome of which is enhanced learning.

Monitoring is an ongoing activity and is integral to teaching and learning. It should not be left to the end of the year. At the same time, 'plans cannot be revised too often or they lose their value as a secure basis for planning' (Fidler, 2002, p. 20). In the process of planning change, teachers need to ask the following questions: Who is monitoring what, in which ways and with what effectiveness? Who is responsible for adjusting what, in which ways, when and with what effectiveness? Resources will need to be allocated appropriately and plans monitored according to the most beneficial use of internal and external expertise.

Monitoring will assist teachers in their planning by providing an insight into the strengths and weaknesses in pupil learning and development and in their own professional practice and knowledge. Effective monitoring requires that each change is monitored in light of its objectives and desired outcome. Everard et al. (2004, p. 30) underline and illustrate some questions that teachers/ schools should consider when developing tools/techniques to measure the effectiveness of an activity/service/facility. The questions on page 96 have been adapted from this and offer a good framework for monitoring specific changes in the classroom.

Monitoring checklist: changes in practice

- How are results used to inform planning and development?
- How might the skills of staff in using evaluation be developed?
- Which outcomes do you wish to measure (for example, changes in behaviour, or attainment etc.)?
- What baseline evidence will be needed? How can this be obtained? What new systems need to be established? Who will be responsible?
- What evidence is there of the 'quality' of this change at different times? How does this inform future development?
- How are the purposes and the results of the evidence collection discussed and shared?
- How reliable or valid is the evidence that is available?
- How is the evidence used and how are results analysed to inform learning in the future?

Monitoring pupil progress

- Have you clearly identified target pupils?
- Do you have robust assessment systems in place?
- Do you use robust tracking systems for each pupil?
- Do you set clear targets for each pupil?
- Do you monitor progress frequently (e.g. half-termly, termly, etc.)?
- Who is monitoring what, in which ways and with what effectiveness?
- How does monitoring and evaluation relate to your overall planning?
- Who is responsible for adjusting what, in which ways, when and with what effectiveness?
- Is everything recorded in writing/online (keeping evidence is important, particularly in the case of children with SEND and the implementation of the Graduated Response; evidence is needed if children go on to need an EHC assessment)?

Evaluation

Evaluation can often proceed simultaneously with the change programme; this should not be left until the end. Hall and Oldroyd (1990) suggest that 'evaluation is a component of development planning and an essential prerequisite to preparing any subsequent plan'. Everard et al. (2004, p. 285) suggest that evaluation will highlight any 'unforeseen consequences of the change', which can subsequently be managed or 'made the subject of further change'. Evaluation is a collaborative exercise that involves:

- asking questions
- gathering information
- forming conclusions

In order to:

- make recommendations.

In contrast to monitoring, evaluation encompasses reviewing and analysing the status of a plan's objectives. Through the evaluation process, teachers/teams will determine the need to change objectives, priorities and/or practice. Hargreaves and Hopkins (1991) and Parsons and Burkey (2011) stress the importance of evaluation (both micro and macro) in enhancing the professional judgment of educators during periods of change. However, essentially, effective evaluation can lead to a change in teachers' perception of their practice.

Evaluation checklist

1. Purposes, broad guidelines, aims or objectives for the subject under scrutiny that are:
   - clear
   - indicators of desired performance or outcomes.
2. Questions that are:
   - unambiguous
   - penetrating
   - useful
   - relevant.
3. Information that is:
   - accessible
   - meaningful
   - related to questions
   - not too voluminous to handle.
4. Conclusions that consider:
   - conditions
   - obstacles and opportunities
   - effects
   - assumptions
   - alternatives.
5. Reports that are:
   - concise
   - informative
   - focused on audience's need
   - likely to inform decision-making.

6. A good evaluation brief:
- specifying much of the above.

(Source: adapted from Hall and Oldroyd, 1990)

The final stage in the evaluation process is to write a report. It is important to consider the purposes of the report as required. Changes can be made for different reasons – for example, for your own professional development and/or to inform the School Improvement Plan, or to address an issue raised in the Ofsted report, which the headteacher wants to explore further with a view to improvement. Essentially, the following aspects of the evaluation process need to be considered:

- Purpose – of the evaluation.
- Content – what is being evaluated?
- Process – how?
- Context – why has the need for evaluation arisen?
- Outcomes – were they achieved? If not, what are the impacts of this, and what could be done differently next time?

Before disseminating the report, reflect on each process and ensure that only necessary and relevant information is presented. Ask the following questions:

---

1. Who monitors the change?
2. How is monitoring carried out?
3. How are all staff kept informed?
4. How is the evaluation carried out?
5. Who prepares the final report?

Evaluation checklist: pupil progress

Impact on pupil learning
Attainment

- Improved test results.
- Learning in other curriculum areas.
- Discernible increases in subject knowledge, understanding and skills.
- Improvements in transferable and key skills.

Dispositions

- The development of more positive attitudes to school and particular subjects.
- Increased motivation to learn.

- Increased confidence and self-esteem.
- Improvement in the quality of relationships.

Metacognition

- Development of self-awareness.
- Increased capacity to reflect on and evaluate their own learning.
- More able to take responsibility for their own learning.

Self-evaluation

All professions are composites of knowledge and understanding, skills and abilities. Self-development involves learning and understanding and a sense of place in relation to job and career. Teachers should have a clear view of what the job is about: the relationship between teaching and management, the school improvement plan and so on. Self-development is systematic; we never stop learning and developing. The art of self-evaluation is to be continually learning. Senge (1990, p. 142) makes it clear:

> *People with a high level of personal mastery are acutely aware of their ignorance, their incompetence, their growth areas. And they are deeply self-confident. Paradoxical? Only for those who do not see that the journey is the reward.*

The culture of the teaching profession and the role of the support staff in schools are changing, reflecting the changing society in which we live, with its proliferation of cultures, beliefs and values. Effective teaching and learning in schools are based on shared beliefs and values. The school community works towards a common goal, reaching for and achieving targets. In practice, staff need to relate their actions to their beliefs and values. If the two do not equate, staff should consider their position in the school in relation to pupils' needs. Schools should be places in which success is celebrated, the 'blame culture' prevalent in the 1980s replaced by the 'caring culture' of the 1990s and beyond. How does this happen? Do teachers willingly participate in the change process, or are they passive in their response to the dominant ideology of the day? Whilst these are matters of sociological debate, self-evaluation and effective self-development should influence practice in a positive way. A starting point for this process could inform practitioners about their individual aspirations in terms of their career. A fundamental issue will be the individual's ability to recognise where they are in relation to where they would like to be.

Theory and knowledge can transform teachers' beliefs and values. In the process of self-reflection, interaction with educational theory may not dictate practice, but it may transform the outlook of the practitioner. Providing individuals with new concepts is a means not merely of offering them a new way of thinking, but also of offering them the possibility of becoming more aware of their thoughts and actions. The full task of self-reflection and evaluation requires teachers to collaborate in decision-making that will transform their situation. The process of self-evaluation encompasses the interaction of teachers with the school.

As a process, self-evaluation should inform practice day to day. An effective professional practitioner will be effective in their evaluation of themselves. In practice, self-evaluation will involve making sense of ourselves in situations. Look at Figure 8 and ask, where am I in this process?

A practice-based approach to self-evaluation is shown in Figure 8. In this example, questions relate to the practitioner making sense of themselves in a range of situations.

Teamwork:	Relationships with:
- listening	- parents
- attitude	- colleagues
- flexibility	- pupils
Knowledge of:	**Preparation of:**
- current publications	- lessons
- equal opportunity issues	- monitoring procedures
- learning styles	- assessment

Self-development checklist: key issues for consideration

- relationship with self (self-evaluation)
- ability to develop
- level of empowerment – status, value
- choices available
- opportunity for individualistic activities.

Self-development involves learning and understanding where you are within your job and career. Teachers should, as stated, have a clear view of what their job is about: the relationship between teaching, leadership and management, the school improvement plan and so on. Teachers should also have an understanding of their position in relation to those they manage. For each member of staff, self-development can be difficult. All staff face many demands, including:

- government demands: to deliver the curriculum, to register pupils, parents' evenings
- senior leadership and management demands: implementation – action of school policy

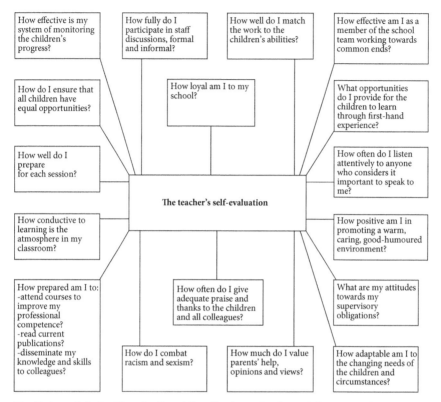

Fig. 8 A model of self-evaluation (Blandford, 2006; adapted from Manchester LEA, 1986)

- colleagues' demands: requests for assistance, information or help from others at a similar level or within your team
- pupils' demands: to inform and liaise
- parents' and governors' demands
- externally imposed demands: social services, police, agencies that work for and with young people
- system-imposed demands: budgets, meetings and social functions, which cannot be ignored.

In addition, there will be other demands such as family, friends, hobbies and social commitments. It is important to understand that teachers and support staff need a balance between their professional and personal lives.

Conclusion

Self-development is ongoing; we never stop learning. And it is important to take ownership of the process, looking for opportunities to develop skills. Evaluation is an essential component of development-planning and an essential prerequisite to preparing any subsequent plan for change. Evaluation is a collaborative exercise involving asking questions, gathering information and forming conclusions in order to make recommendations. Monitoring allows you to track the progress of the plan as it is going forward and to make changes if it is not achieving expected outcomes at each stage. And most significantly, monitoring will provide a framework in which teachers can reflect on their own practice, an outcome of which is enhanced job satisfaction.

Chapter 6 takeaway

Teaching tip

Identify the 20 per cent lowest achieving pupils in your class. Consider how you currently monitor their progress. Take time to reflect on how you could do this better.

Pass it on

Develop a monitoring and evaluation group. Bring together a group of colleagues from your school and other local schools. Discuss how you monitor pupil progress and how you evaluate pupil learning. How could you do this better?

Share and tweet

Using the series hashtag #BloomsCPD share the following: effective monitoring and evaluation leads to enhanced classroom practice and better outcomes for pupils.

CPD book club recommendation

Read some of the research evaluation reports on the Department for Education website. Available at publications (use 'evaluation' as the keyword in the search box): https://www.gov.uk/government/publications?keywords=&publication_filter_option=all&topics%5B%5D=all&departments%5B%5D=department-for-education&official_document_status=all&world_locations%5B%5D=all&from_date=&to_date=

Professional Development Manual: A Practical Guide to Planning and Evaluating Successful Staff Development by Sonia Blandford (see bibliography).

Bloggers' corner

There are few blogs on effective monitoring and evaluation of a change made in classroom practice/pedagogy. Consider writing a blog for the Chartered College of Teaching on effective monitoring and evaluation of classroom change.

TO DO LIST:

☐ Read *Professional Development Manual: A Practical Guide to Planning and Evaluating Successful Staff Development*.

☐ Reflect on how you could better use both monitoring and evaluation to improve pupil outcomes (it will be helpful to do a gap analysis and find out about good pupil data-tracking systems).

☐ Discuss with colleagues how you could further develop this collaboratively.

7 Self-evaluation questionnaire

The previous chapter considered the centrality of monitoring, evaluation and self-reflection in developing your practice, yourself and raising attainment in the classroom. If approaches and activities are not monitored or evaluated, you cannot know accurately how effective they have been – that is, have the desired outcomes been achieved? This chapter follows on from the previous chapter in that it asks you to reflect on your own practice in the context of raising attainment in the classroom. It asks you to reflect on what you have learnt or changed or improved through reading this book and working through the practical exercises presented. The intention is to enable you to get better at what you do by self-evaluating your practices, approaches and values; as with all professionals, teachers are continually learning and improving. For as Senge (1990) makes it clear: 'People with a high level of personal mastery live in a continual learning mode. They never "arrive".' (p. 142)

You will remember the questionnaire process from Chapter 2; this chapter follows a similar format, but here is a reminder of the approaches you can take.

Quick response approach

If your preference for the self-evaluation is to go with your gut only, then simply fill in the quick response section after each question with the first thing that comes into your mind when you ask yourself the question. Do not mull over the question too carefully; simply read thoroughly and answer quickly. This approach will give you an overview of your current understanding and practice of raising attainment in the primary classroom and will take relatively little time. Just make sure you are uninterrupted, in a quiet place and able to complete the questionnaire in one sitting with no distractions so that you get focused and honest answers.

Considered response approach

If you choose to take a more reflective and detailed approach, then you can leave the quick response section blank and go straight on to reading the further guidance section under each question. This guidance provides prompt questions and ideas to get you thinking in detail about the question being answered and is designed to open up a wider scope in your answer. It will also enable you to look at your experience and pull examples into your answer to back up your statements. You may want to complete a few questions at a time and take breaks, or you may be prepared to sit and work through the questions all in one sitting to ensure you remain focused. This approach does take longer, but it can lead to a more in-depth understanding of your current practice, and you will gain more from the process than the quick response alone.

Combined approach

A thorough approach, and one I recommend, would be to use both approaches together regardless of personal preference. There is clear value in both approaches being used together. This would involve you firstly answering the self-evaluation quick response questions by briefly noting down your instinctual answers for all questions. The next step would be to return to the start of the self-evaluation, read the further guidance and then answer the questions once more, slowly and in detail, forming more of a narrative around each question and pulling in examples from your own experience. Following this you would need to read over both responses and form a comprehensive and honest summary in your mind of your answers and a final view of where you feel you stand right now in your CPD.

This is the longest of the three approaches to this questionnaire but will give you a comprehensive and full understanding of your current practice, thoughts and feelings in relation to raising attainment in the primary classroom.
You will be surprised at the difference you see between the quick response and the considered response answers to the same questions. It can be very illuminating.

- I have done this self-assessment before.
- I only want a surface-level overview of my current understanding and practice.
- I work better when I work at speed.
- I don't have much time.

Quick

- I have never done this self-assessment before.
- I want a deeper understanding of my current understanding and practice.
- I work better when I take my time and really think things over.
- I have some time to do this self-assessment.

Considered

- I have never done this self-assessment before.
- I have done this self-assessment before.
- I want a comprehensive and full understanding of my current understanding and practice and want to compare that to what I thought before taking the self-assessment.
- I have a decent amount of time to dedicate to completing this self-assessment.

Combined

Fig. 9 How should I approach the self-assessment questionnaire?

Rating	Definition
1	Not at all. I don't. None at all. Not happy. Not confident at all.
2	Rarely. Barely. Very little. Very unconfident.
3	Not often at all. Not much. Quite unconfident.
4	Not particularly. Not really. Not a lot. Mildly unconfident.
5	Neutral. Unsure. Don't know. Indifferent.
6	Sometimes. At times. Moderately. A little bit. Mildly confident.
7	Quite often. A fair bit. Some. A little confident.
8	Most of the time. More often than not. Quite a lot. Quite confident.
9	The majority of the time. A lot. Very confident.
10	Completely. Very much so. A huge amount. Extremely happy. Extremely confident.

Fig. 10 Rate yourself definitions

Rate yourself

The final part of the self-evaluation is to rate yourself. This section will ask you to rate your confidence and happiness in each area that has been covered in the questionnaire with a view to working on these areas for improvement. The table above shows how the scale works: the higher the number you allocate yourself, the better you feel you are performing in that area.

Raising attainment in the primary classroom: self-assessment questionnaire

QUESTION 1: What new things have you considered or tried that you have liked in terms of raising attainment in the classroom?

Quick response:

_____

_____

_____

_____

Questions for consideration

- How did you initiate/implement them?
- Have the children reacted to the change?
- Have they been effective?

Considered response:

_____

_____

_____

_____

_____

Rate yourself

QUESTION 1: How happy are you that you've tried all you wanted to try for raising attainment in the classroom?

1   2   3   4   5   6   7   8   9   10

QUESTION 2: What changes have you made that you feel have had an impact upon children's attainment in your classroom?

Quick response:

_____

_____

_____

_____

Questions for consideration

- What did you change/do differently?
- Has it improved children's outcomes?
- Are children more engaged?
- Has it had an impact on certain groups of children (those with SEN or Pupil Premium children)?

Considered response:

_____

_____

_____

_____

_____

_____

_____

_____

Rate yourself

QUESTION 2: How much impact on children's attainment do you feel you've had?

1	2	3	4	5	6	7	8	9	10

QUESTION 3: How would you now describe your general approach to raising attainment?

Quick response:

_____

_____

_____

_____

Questions for consideration

- Do you monitor children's performance data more closely?
- Do you talk to children more about their learning?
- Do you discuss with colleagues at the planning stage how perceived difficult areas of the curriculum can be taught?

Considered response:

_____

_____

_____

_____

_____

_____

_____

_____

_____

_____

_____

Rate yourself

QUESTION 3: How happy are you with your approach to raising attainment in the classroom?

| 1 | 2 | 3 | 4 | 5 | 6 | 7 | 8 | 9 | 10 |

QUESTION 4: What educational theories, research, ideas or case studies do you have an interest in and how do they inform your practice?

Quick response:

_____

_____

_____

_____

Questions for consideration

- How have the case studies in Chapter 5 informed your practice?
- What piece of research you have read about in this book has influenced how you approach raising attainment?
- Have you discussed research relating to raising attainment with your colleagues? (Have you formed a research group?)
- How could you or your school better use research evidence to inform your practice?
- Have you carried out your own research?

Considered response:

_____

_____

_____

_____

_____

_____

Rate yourself

QUESTION 4: How confident are you with your knowledge of educational research?

1	2	3	4	5	6	7	8	9	10

QUESTION 5: What have you shared or discussed regarding raising attainment with colleagues?

Quick response:

_____

_____

_____

_____

Questions for consideration

- Have you discussed your experiences of change in practice or approach with colleagues?
- Do you have regular data-led (pupil data) discussions with colleagues?
- Do you share practice/observation/other with colleagues in other local schools?

Considered response:

_____

_____

_____

_____

_____

_____

_____

_____

_____

_____

Rate yourself

QUESTION 5: How confident are you about sharing your ideas with others?

| 1 | 2 | 3 | 4 | 5 | 6 | 7 | 8 | 9 | 10 |

QUESTION 6: Where do you feel your strengths now lie in raising attainment in the classroom?

Quick response:

_____

_____

_____

_____

Questions for consideration

- What are your strengths with regard to raising attainment?
- Have you developed different approaches/techniques to raising the attainment of children with SEND, Pupil Premium children and others at risk of underachievement?
- Have you developed strategies to stretch the more able pupils?

Considered response:

_____

_____

_____

_____

_____

_____

_____

_____

_____

Rate yourself

QUESTION 6: How confident are you when it comes to your raising attainment practice?

| 1 | 2 | 3 | 4 | 5 | 6 | 7 | 8 | 9 | 10 |

QUESTION 7: Where do you feel your weaknesses now lie in raising attainment?

Quick response:

_____

_____

_____

_____

Questions for consideration

- Have you developed your subject knowledge?
- Have you developed your pedagogical knowledge?
- Have you and your colleagues carried out peer observation of lessons and feedback?

Considered response:

_____

_____

_____

_____

_____

_____

_____

_____

_____

_____

Rate yourself

QUESTION 7: How serious do you feel your weaknesses are when it comes to raising attainment in the classroom?

1   2   3   4   5   6   7   8   9   10

QUESTION 8: What approaches would you like to try that you have not already?

Quick response:

_____

_____

_____

_____

Questions for consideration

- Have you had discussions with colleagues about changing practices or approaches?
- Have you looked closely at your personal targets and considered how you could make changes based on them?
- Have you engaged with the research base and considered how the researchers initiated change in their practice?

Considered response:

_____

_____

_____

_____

_____

_____

_____

_____

_____

Rate yourself

QUESTION 8: How confident are you when it comes to trying something new?

1	2	3	4	5	6	7	8	9	10

QUESTION 9: Is there anything that is holding you back in developing your attainment-raising practice?

Quick response:

_____

_____

_____

_____

Questions for consideration

- What area of raising attainment do you want to improve on (consider across leadership of learning, teaching and learning, parent and carer engagement and wider opportunities for children)?
- Where are the gaps in your training?
- Are you familiar with all school policies and government policies relating to raising attainment?

Considered response:

_____

_____

_____

_____

_____

_____

_____

_____

_____

Rate yourself

QUESTION 9: How confident do you feel you are not being held back?

1   2   3   4   5   6   7   8   9   10

QUESTION 10: Is there anything that you have tried in the classroom as a result of using this book so far?

Quick response:

_____

_____

_____

_____

Questions for consideration

- Have you reflected on the place of aspirations and an aspirational outlook for all children and how you communicate this to the children?
- Have you reflected on any barriers to learning each child may have and how you can start to deconstruct the barriers in the classroom?
- Do you give children more opportunity to reflect on their learning through discussion and self-evaluation?
- Do children know the 'how' of learning?

Considered response:

_____

_____

_____

_____

_____

_____

_____

_____

Rate yourself

QUESTION 10: How confident do you feel in trying out new approaches to raising attainment in the classroom?

1	2	3	4	5	6	7	8	9	10

QUESTION 11: Do you have an understanding of what children think about your strategies for raising attainment?

Quick response:

_____

_____

_____

_____

Questions for consideration

- Have you asked children their views on the changes you have made?
- Have you asked the children to compare what it was like before and what it is like now?
- Have you noticed changes in pupil attainment and progress?

Considered response:

_____

_____

_____

_____

_____

_____

_____

_____

_____

Rate yourself

QUESTION 11: How confident are you that you really know what students think about your strategies for raising attainment?

1	2	3	4	5	6	7	8	9	10

QUESTION 12: How have you interacted with parents and carers concerning their child's attainment?

Quick response:

_____

_____

_____

_____

Questions for consideration

- Have you considered how you can involve parents and carers who are not involved in the school or engaged in their child's learning?
- Have you arranged workshops for parents and carers on what their children are learning in class?
- Do you consider the parents' views when you are setting targets for children's learning?

Considered response:

_____

_____

_____

_____

_____

_____

_____

_____

_____

Rate yourself

QUESTION 12: How confident are you about interacting with parents and carers?

1	2	3	4	5	6	7	8	9	10

The results

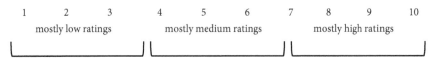

Fig. 11 How did you rate yourself?

Mostly low ratings

You have made a start, but still have some way to go with your approach to raising attainment. It may be a good idea to do a self-analysis of your strengths, challenges and areas for further development. Then develop an action plan of how you will go about closing the gaps for yourself. This book provides good guidance and support for improving your practice to raise the attainment of all children. Revisit the areas in the book related to the areas in your practice you have identified as being less strong.

Mostly medium ratings

You will have started putting some of the approaches and practices discussed in this book into practice. You will have noticed some impact on pupil attainment. Keep going. You are doing well. But now it is time to move forward. Use the book to identify areas you feel need further development and actively make the changes. You need to enhance or polish your skills.

Mostly high ratings

Now is the time to go from good to great. Well done so far. It is good at this stage to consider how you can raise attainment even more. What could you do to further close the attainment gap for the children at risk of underachievement and what could you do to further stretch the most able children? We sometimes hear the expression 'the forgotten middle', the children in the middle attainment bracket. These are the children to focus on. Perhaps there are one or two little changes you could make in your teaching that would make a big difference to their outcomes.

Now what?

Through the many reflective activities you will have worked through in this book, it is time to start thinking about how you can embed some of the practices and approaches in your teaching. You are the leader of learning in the classroom and how you do this will have a significant impact on children's learning, development and outcomes. Thinking about leadership, how you lead and how you can do this better is an important aspect of teaching. The following chapter considers leadership, what it means, characteristics of good leaders and how, through good leadership, you can get the best possible outcomes for every child.

Chapter 7 takeaway

Teaching tip

We never stop learning and improving. Continue to reflect objectively on your practice (knowledge and pedagogy). Aim to do it every half term and use the questions in this book as the framework.

Pass it on

Consider developing a school blog and ask colleagues to contribute a post (one a week) relating in some way to raising attainment in the classroom. You could also extend this to getting other local schools to take part.

Share and tweet

Share your thoughts on how this book has helped you to raise attainment in the classroom using the hashtag #BloomsCPD.

CPD book club recommendation

Children, Their World, Their Education: Final Report and Recommendations of the Cambridge Primary Review edited by Robin Alexander

This book and the research papers published alongside it relate closely to raising attainment in the primary classroom.

Bloggers' corner

Look up the various blogs mentioned in the previous chapters and consider what view you want your blog posts to have. Are you going to publish all blogs sent to you by colleagues? Or are you going to have certain criteria that writers must adhere to?

TO DO LIST:

❑ Put dates in your diary of when you are going to review and evaluate your practice in the coming year. The self-reflection questions in Chapter 5, those in this chapter and those in Chapter 2 are helpful.

❑ At this stage do a gap analysis of your strengths and weaknesses. Consider how you are going to build on your strengths and develop your weaker areas.

❑ Read the book *Children, Their World, Their Education: Final Report and Recommendations of the Cambridge Primary Review* edited by Robin Alexander.

❑ Write the first blog and invite other colleagues to write forthcoming blogs.

8

Embedding and developing practice

Every teacher is a leader. Leading learning in the classroom will involve change; it is founded on raised aspirations (teachers, leaders, pupils, parents and other school staff) and increased access to learning leading to achievement for all. Leadership development, across four key areas – vision, commitment, communication and collaboration – and how this is borne out in practice will determine the extent to which effective practices and approaches are developed and become embedded in the class and school systems.

The development of school leaders underpins current government policy to improve outcomes for all children. Good leadership is an art that can be developed, and includes working effectively with others, delegating responsibility and building strong teams. Leaders and would-be leaders can learn to lead and develop a style appropriate to their personal characteristics, which is adapted to the context in which they operate. In essence, the skills required for effective leadership can be developed and enhanced by working within frameworks for good practice.

This chapter will focus on 'every teacher a leader' and support you in considering effective ways of developing your own capacity for leadership, where the focus is always on raising attainment and getting the best outcomes for pupils. In so doing, you will be better placed to support other colleagues in their professional development. Before you get into this chapter, it is worth reflecting on your own personal and professional qualities. It will help you to focus better on leadership and what it means to you now and going forward.

Considering your personal and professional qualities

- What do you enjoy about your work?
- What do you find less enjoyable?
- What do you value in terms of raising the attainment of all children?
- Are these values in line with your school's values?
- Do you feel you have a strong impact on the children's learning and development?
- In what ways do you think you could have more of an impact on children's learning and development?
- Do you engage with government education policy?
- Do you engage with current research evidence?
- Do you do your own action research?
- What could you change in your job to make it more enjoyable?
- What could you do in your job to make it more manageable (in terms of time)?
- Do you have the ability to self-manage?

- Do you have clear personal objectives (for your ongoing professional development)?
- Do you place an emphasis on continuing personal growth?
- Do you have effective problem-solving skills?
- Do you have the capacity to be creative and innovative?

Defining leadership

There are many definitions of **leadership** in educational and business literature. Blandford (2006, pp. 4, 10) defines leadership in terms of practice as the 'achievement of objectives through people, [where leaders are] those with power and influence'. This can be compared and contrasted with management, where managers sustain an existing code or model of practice, with limited authority to change the 'direction' or 'objectives' of an organisation. This is not to be confused with the management of people, where the role of the leader will also include the management of colleagues. In fact, the essentials of good leadership hinge on the effective and appropriate management of people.

It is widely acknowledged within the field of education that effective school leaders contribute to the development of effective schools. Jones and Pound (2008, p. 2) conclude that: '... the quality of leadership and management is paramount in determining the extent to which a setting meets young children's individual needs'.

At this stage, it is worth reflecting on the following characteristics of good leadership.

Checklist: characteristics of good leadership

- Recognising and acting upon relevant information; listen and learn.
- Developing a style of leadership appropriate to the individual and the task.
- Being forceful and not dictatorial. Being decisive when necessary and driving things along, whilst remaining sensitive to team members. Keeping abreast of initiatives and preparing the team for future developments. In addition, securing the commitment and trust of the team.
- Recognising the tasks that can be delegated, and how they can be delegated best.
- Motivating the team by identifying the areas that individuals find satisfying, developmental and rewarding, and providing individuals with meaningful work.

However, leadership (and management) is not a straightforward activity. Whilst more than a decade old, the conclusions of Fidler (2002, p. 32) (who has written widely on educational management) are worth bearing in mind when considering leadership in schools and settings:

Leadership is a complex area with many apparently contradictory requirements. Suggestions that particular approaches to leadership should be universal ... should be resisted ... Leadership will need to exhibit many actions in different styles on different occasions.

Carol Stephenson (former Dean of the Ivey Business School in London, Ontario) (2005) suggests that the common trait of effective leaders is that they are 'collaborative and receptive to the ideas and views of others'.

Similarly, a school leader is responsible for collaborating with, and interpreting the work of, others:

- local and national policies
- staff, parents and children who are divided into teams – according to task
- practitioners (from teaching and nursing backgrounds), non-teaching and support staff (including those from multi-disciplinary teams – family support workers, health personnel such as speech therapists, psychologists, etc.)
- their own team leaders – in order to achieve and communicate excellence, through their own learning, to a diverse and informed audience – practitioners/teachers, parents and multi-agency team leaders.

Leaders should also consider how their practice is informed by their vision and how this informs organisational practice. Blandford and Knowles (2013, p. 40) note that vision in education settings should be ' ... achievement-orientated, inspirational, and aspirational and, as such, should be shared by all members of the school'.

Developing teams

The opportunity to participate in decision-making teams that impact on the effectiveness of an organisation is becoming more commonplace in education, where the government promotes the development of school networks to share good practice. This approach is also reflected in the number of networks that have developed at local and national level. You may already be involved in some of these networks and/or lead them. But it is worth considering how you can develop and lead a group of colleagues within your school.

Effective teams

In developing effective teams, it is important to be aware that teams do not act as teams simply because they are described as such. Everard et al, (2004, p. 163) defined a team as:

... a group of people with common objectives that can effectively tackle any task which it has been set to do. The contribution drawn from each member is of the highest possible quality, and is one which could not have been called into play other than in the context of a supportive team.

Team leadership has attracted many commentators and academics. Northouse (2004, p. 210), a respected author in the field of leadership, particularly relating theory to practice, emphasised the need for team leaders to focus on 'what makes teams effective or what constitutes team excellence'. He suggested that leaders cannot improve groups without a clear focus on team goals or outcomes. Employing the criteria for group effectiveness proposed by Hackman and Walton (1986) of Harvard University, USA and characteristics for team excellence proposed by Larson and LaFasto (1989), Northouse (2004, pp. 211–215) proposed the following framework (adapted below) for developing an effective team:

- Clear elevating goals – the team should be kept focused on the goals, and outcomes can be evaluated against the objectives.
- Results-driven structure – teams should find the best structure to accomplish their goals.
- Competent team members – team members need to be provided with the appropriate information and training to carry out their job effectively and to be able to work collaboratively within the team
- Unified commitment – effective teams do not just happen. They are carefully designed and developed. Involving team members in the various processes can enhance the sense of unity.
- Collaborative climate – founded on trust, out of which develops honesty, openness, consistency and respect, where integration of individual actions is seen as one of the fundamental characteristics of effective teams.
- Standards of excellence – need to be clear and concrete, where team members feel a certain pressure to perform well. An effective leader can facilitate this process by: requiring results – make expectations clear; reviewing results – provide feedback to resolve performance issues; and rewarding results – acknowledge superior performance.
- External support and recognition – provide teams with the necessary resources to carry out the required tasks and reward team member performance, rather than individual achievement.
- Leadership of effective teams – leaders influence teams through four processes: cognitive – helps the team to understand the problems with which they are confronted; motivational – unites the team and helps the members to achieve the required standards; affective – helps the team to cope with difficult situations by providing clear goals, assignments and strategies; and co-ordination – matches individual skills to roles, provides clear objectives, monitors feedback and adapts to changes.

Building the team

Developing team skills will involve a balance between concern for team, concern for the task and developing the individual. Few leaders are able to achieve this effective balance. Everard et al. (2004, p. 163) highlight the 'ineffective way tasks are handled' when teams do not 'gel'. Referring to educational settings, they further suggest that 'when... groups... fail to work at peak efficiency the effectiveness of the whole organisation suffers'. A team leader may find identifying the characteristics of his/her team difficult. The nature of the task and the ethos of the school will influence the working habits of team members. Equally, pressure from external agencies will affect the quality of the team. Family commitments, hobbies and political initiatives are areas of influence on leaders' lives; these, in turn, will influence the individual's commitment to the team. In essence, the quality of the relationships within the team will determine the quality of the task.

Teachers should aim to lead and participate in effective teams that agree aims, share skills, realise potential and reduce stress and anxiety. A leader should avoid the pitfalls of weak management, which include:

- overemphasis on people
- overemphasis on task
- overemphasis on agendas, not processes
- reacting to events, not anticipating them
- failure to celebrate success, individual and team.

Teams do not act as teams because they are described as such. Effective teams require essential elements to make them work. Reflect on the following, adapted from West (1995, p. 127), which provides a framework for building an effective team.

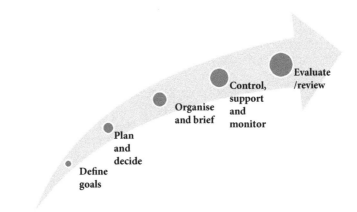

Fig. 12 Developing a team

Mentoring

Mentoring is a widely recognised means of enabling staff to develop both individually and as team members. Mentoring generally means the positive support offered by staff with some experience to staff with less experience. This experience can extend over a wide range of activities or be specific to one activity. Mentoring will differ according to need and includes enhancing the mentee's skills and professional development, helping to develop a set of educational values, consulting to help the mentee to clarify goals and ways of implementing them, helping to establish a set of personal and professional standards, and networking and sponsoring by providing opportunities for the mentee to meet other professionals.

Although mentoring is time-consuming, it provides an effective approach to staff professional development. Mentees should select their mentor based on professional needs, present and/or future. It is important to understand that mentoring is a continuous staff development activity, which, once the system is established, takes place during the normal day-to-day life of the school. Mentors need to know and understand the essential elements of a mentoring relationship. The following provides a useful summary of the essential features of the mentoring process:

- a recognised procedure, formal or informal
- a clear understanding of the procedure and the roles of mentor and mentee
- trust and a rapport between both parties
- the credibility and genuineness of the mentor as perceived by the mentee
- confidentiality and discretion
- a relationship based on the mentee's perception of his/her own needs
- a suitable range of skills used by the mentor: counselling, listening, sensitive questioning, analysis and handing back responsibilities
- an appropriate attitude from both parties, for example the ability of the mentor to challenge the mentee, and the self-motivation of the mentee to take action when necessary
- in addition, teachers should be aware of equal opportunity issues that need to be addressed in the selection and training of mentors.

Leadership behaviour

In practice, the way leaders and their teams behave is dependent on numerous factors (including those intrinsic to the leader/team, for example, personal qualities, and extrinsic factors, such as relevant training), which influence individuals and impact on the lives of the people they contact. One important aspect of leadership is that of motivating those who work within your team. By examining various acknowledged models of motivation, this section will consider how this might be effectively carried out in practice.

Motivation

Motivation (that being inspiring others to do/carry out and to want to do/carry out what is required or needed) is central to good leadership. Effective team leaders involve all staff within their team in influencing the quality of learning, teaching and achievement. Team leaders should have knowledge and understanding of how to provide all members with meaningful and productive work. Good team leaders should have little difficulty in identifying the teaching and learning elements that colleagues find satisfying and rewarding or challenging. Identification of motivational factors beyond the team might be more difficult. In brief, several models of 'motivation' exist, which can be summarised as follows (from *Writers on Organisations*, Pugh and Hickson, 1989):

The social model (Mayo, 1933):

- people are motivated by social needs, friendship and acceptance; their basic sense of identity is formed through relationships with other people
- people are responsive to peer group pressure
- people are responsive to management if management meets their needs (belonging, etc.).

The rational-economic model (Taylor, 1947):

- people act to maximise their financial and material rewards
- people will perform specialised tasks for high rewards.

Self-actualising model (Maslow, 1943):

- hierarchical needs (i.e. to progress to a higher position within their organisation)
- people work to develop skills
- people are self-motivated and self-controlled
- people will integrate their goals with those of the organisation.

Maslow (1943), the American psychologist renowned for his 'hierarchy of needs' theory (see table on page 131), provides an introduction to the analysis of human behaviour. Maslow suggested that there are five levels of need that influence an individual's behaviour:

• physiological needs	food, drink and shelter
• safety needs	protection against danger, threat and deprivation
• social needs	to associate, have relationships, affection, belonging
• ego needs	self-esteem, reputation, status
• self-actualisation	the need for realising one's own potential for continual self-development

According to Maslow, the needs hierarchy means that the lower-order needs have to be satisfied before the other needs become a goal or a paramount need. In behavioural terms these levels determine the needs that motivate individuals (see Figure 13).

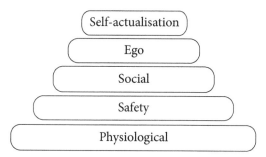

Fig. 13 Maslow's Hierarchy of Needs (Maslow, 1943)

Essentially, teachers will have needs, for, as Maslow (1943, p. 382) stated, 'A musician must make music, an artist must paint, a poet must write, if he is to be ultimately happy [...] This need we may call self-actualization'. In theory, when these needs are satisfied, the individual will be happy and motivated in their work.

Conclusion

The impact, importance and centrality of effective leadership in schools is widely acknowledged. Effective leaders in education contribute to, and lead, the development of effective educational organisations. Enabling teachers to develop and grow as leaders is vital for their own professional development and development of education across the country. Below is a summary of how the development of leadership skills, effective teamwork and mentoring contribute to raising the attainment of all pupils.

Raising attainment in the classroom and across the school: leadership, mentoring and teamwork

- **Developing leadership skills helps you to lead learning better in the classroom:** managing pupils and their learning, tracking data, assessing pupil progress and attainment, monitoring and evaluating, engaging parents and developing wider opportunities for the pupils. At the same time, it helps you to consider your own professional path.

- **Development through mentoring:** mentoring develops both the mentor and mentee; both have to focus on practice and improvement. It often works best when an experienced teacher is the mentor of a less experienced teacher. The focus should be on practices and approaches that raise attainment in the classroom.
- **Development through teamwork:** team meetings provide a platform on which many points of view are heard; this provides an opportunity to hear about alternative approaches and practices. Many meetings in schools will focus on planning, assessment, data and other aspects relating to best practice to raise attainment. They provide an opportunity to develop your own practice, as part of a team, with the support of the team.

Part two of this book looks at how you can further develop yourself as a leader by leading other colleagues in their own professional practice and in getting better outcomes for every child.

Chapter 8 takeaway

Teaching tip

Make a plan on an A4 piece of paper (hard/soft copy) of how you would develop and train a team within your school to lead a number of professional development sessions over a term on raising attainment in the primary classroom. (Who would join? What are the challenges/ strengths? What ground rules need to be established, etc.?)

Pass it on

How would you expand your group to include teachers from other local schools? How could you support your group model to develop as networks across England?

Share and tweet

Using the series hashtag #BloomsCPD select one key thing/ thought you have learnt about leading learning in the classroom and across the school.

CPD book club recommendation

Middle Leadership in Schools: Harmonising Leadership and Learning by Sonia Blandford (see bibliography).

This book looks at middle leadership in schools and addresses all the common challenges that leaders and managers face. In a step-by-step approach, it shows the reader how to turn challenges to strengths and develop leadership practice to raise the attainment of children.

Bloggers' corner

Read the blogs on the National College for Teaching and Leadership website. Available at: https://nctl.blog.gov.uk/about/

TO DO LIST:

☐ Develop a staff team to lead CPD sessions on raising attainment in the primary classroom (you will need to make an action plan and consider who is doing what, when and how).

☐ Discuss with colleagues how you could further develop this collaboratively to a network of schools.

☐ Read *Middle Leadership in Schools* by Sonia Blandford.

☐ Check out the National College for Teaching and Leadership website and find a couple of blogposts that interest you.

Part 2

Train others

1 Preparing for CPD

This chapter provides a few thoughts on developing, planning and implementing CPD programmes for teachers in your school and beyond, founded on the principles of attainment for all. When CPD is effective, participants can expect the following:

- a more confident grasp of knowledge (in issues related to attainment for all)
- a heightened awareness of different teaching methods
- a sharper approach to matching work to children's or young people's needs
- more effective questioning techniques
- better curriculum documentation
- closer collaboration between support staff and teachers.

This chapter will show you how to develop effective CPD for raising the attainment of all children and young people.

What is professional development?

Professional development is the development of teachers and support staff to enhance their knowledge and understanding, skills and abilities, and quality of teaching and learning to get better outcomes for all children. In practice, development is a term encompassing any experience or process that helps to bring out an individual's full potential.

As a manager and teacher your aim is to improve the quality of your own practice and that of your staff. You will be responsible for achieving targets and will only succeed if the people who work with you are competent as well. This chapter gives you examples of how you can take your own professional development and that of your colleagues to higher levels.

In a learning community, staff development will include personal development, team development and school development. In addition to developing individual skills, staff development has a wider importance in:

- promoting shared values (e.g. high aspirations for children)
- implementing change (e.g. engaging with research)
- promoting equal opportunities (e.g. giving more 'prime' time to children at risk of underachievement).

In general, managers, leaders, teachers and practitioners have a shared responsibility to see that individuals develop new skills. It is critical to note that staff development should not mean an additional activity. Staff development should be integral to school development.

Checklist: what is professional development?

Professional development involves:

- working with staff to identify professional needs
- planning, organising and facilitating programmes that improve staff effectiveness and are consistent with school goals and needs
- supervising individuals and groups
- providing feedback on performance
- providing a remedy for ineffective teaching
- participating in recruitment and development activities
- initiating self-development.

Professional development encompasses:

- **Practitioner development:** school-based development, self-development, induction, mentoring, observation, job shadowing and team teaching.
- **Professional education:** award-bearing courses managed and taught at higher education institutions, focusing on the relationship between educational theory and practice.
- **Professional training:** conferences, courses and workshops that emphasise practical information and skills.
- **Professional support:** the responsibility of colleagues in school, through the process of fulfilling contractual conditions of service, e.g. recruitment and selection procedures encompassing job descriptions, promotion, career development, performance management, mentoring, team-building, redeployment and job opportunities.

(Source: adapted from Bolam, 1993)

Linking school and professional development

If the development, implementation, monitoring and evaluation of school effectiveness are to be successful, staff need to be trained. Collaboration in school promotes discussion. Professional development and school development should be planned together. At the same time, in the context of the drive to raise standards, senior managers and leaders have become increasingly aware of the tensions that can exist between individual and whole-school needs.

Senior and middle leaders and managers need to consider staff development when setting targets for school development. Participation in staff development is critical to both individual and school success. A school's professional development policy will both reflect the aims of the school strategic (based on vision or mission) and developmental plan and meet individual needs.

A guiding model for a professional development school indicates the need for teaching and non-teaching staff to have a range of knowledge and understanding, skills and abilities to meet the needs of their pupils; these include subject knowledge, teaching and learning styles, elements of learning attitudes, areas of classroom practice, assessment and data-recording (and analysis). The latter is important in the context of closely monitoring the progress and attainment of your pupils. Training and development needs to be relevant, broad, balanced, differentiated and reflected in the school development plan. Personal and professional development are directly related to school development; but a note of caution – too much emphasis on meeting school needs can deskill and demotivate teachers and support staff, and lead to staff wastage.

Leaders and managers should reflect on the choices available within the following context (this can also provide the framework for doing a self-audit of professional development needs):

- What is required to improve performance?
- How will this be done?
- When will this be done?

A model for school and staff development starts with the role of the school, as stated in the mission and vision statements and the aims. This leads to the school development plan, which encompasses a supporting professional development policy that includes the performance management process. This then leads to staff development that responds to national, local and school goals in order to get the best outcomes for pupils through improvements in the curriculum and teaching and learning. Critically, staff development leads to personal and professional growth and strengthens any areas of weaker performance. In the context of an operational plan, there is a need to set objectives, assign responsibilities, enlist participation, provide incentives, allocate resources, plan professional development activities and monitor and evaluate impact (with a view to revising and adapting as needed).

Checklist: what does professional development for raising attainment look like?

Professional development for raising attainment involves:

- opportunity to reflect on what you know and do already and your gaps (subject knowledge, pedagogical knowledge and wider practice)

- opportunity to consider specific and common teaching and learning issues
- time to understand and reflect on the rationale behind new ideas/research
- opportunity to try out new ideas/approaches and consider whether they will work in your particular context/school
- opportunity to gain new expertise (e.g. observing other teachers)
- opportunity to get feedback and coaching on your own practice.

Performance management: keeping records

Performance management is an essential element in the development of teachers and practitioners. Its purpose is to provide an opportunity for performance enhancement that motivates and develops individuals. When it is implemented effectively and linked with the school improvement plan, it can enhance the overall performance of the school.

Performance management and review should improve the quality of education for children by enabling teachers to realise their potential and to carry out their duties more effectively.

Checklist: what is the purpose of performance review?

The purpose of performance is:

- To raise standards through target setting that enhances teacher performance, and to improve provision for children.
- To link the review cycle to:
  - local development plans
  - school management procedures
  - Ofsted – action plan
  - annual reviews and development plans
  - individual staff development plans
  - induction and assessment
  - planning the professional development of the school workforce within the national, local and school frameworks.

A working definition of performance review is one professional holding him/herself accountable to him/herself in the presence of another professional. The review may improve the management of teaching and learning within the school by helping teachers to identify ways of enhancing their skills and performance and supporting them in the identification of achievable targets. Performance review should assist in planning professional development individually and collectively within the framework set by the school improvement plan. In addition, this will enhance the overall management of the school and provide an opportunity to consider the management of change. Performance review should also support the promotion of equal opportunities.

To this end, a performance review is open and based on the mutual understanding by all staff within the school of its context, purpose, procedures, criteria and outcomes. The process and procedures adopted should be fair and equitable and should be seen to be so, both in general and by respecting equal opportunities. The process and procedures supporting performance review should also be acceptable to all staff. The school workforce should benefit from participation in the scheme. There should be the opportunity for objective judgements to be made concerning the management of the institution.

The scheme should be integral to the school's development strategy and attempt to balance the demands of professional development and public accountability. A rigorous system of review is one that raises standards, key elements of which are trust, training, resourcing, time, support and commitment. For performance management to have any meaning it should be seen to inform the school development process. To this end, schools should aim to have in place a co-ordinated procedure for ensuring that:

- mechanisms exist for collating professional development needs identified through individual reviews
- there is co-ordination of training needs and related development opportunities
- there are contingency plans for coping with those whose performance is perceived as poor for a variety of reasons, e.g. stress, lack of skills.

As performance review is an annual process, there is an opportunity to agree targets with staff in the light of targets within the school development plan, which will itself be influenced by key points for action in Ofsted reports and benchmark information from national data (e.g. DfE performance data).

Action planning

An action plan is the link between training and follow up. It is the implementation process that links new learning to practice in the school and classroom. For a personal action plan, the starting point is an audit of your strengths and areas of challenge, in the context of your performance review (but not exclusively). The following checklist will help you identify your personal training needs:

Checklist: identification of personal training needs

You can use a combination of the following to assess your own training needs:

- recording and analysing daily activities
- seeking the observations and comments of colleagues
- asking a senior leader/manager to appraise a particular aspect of your performance
- considering likely career paths and identifying the skills gap
- keeping a personal diary of management experiences.

Your action plan should contain:

- agreed priority areas (some from performance review and others you may have identified from the above list)
- targets – specific objectives for the priority area
- success *criteria* against which your progress and achievement can be judged
- the tasks to be undertaken
- allocation of responsibility for tasks and targets – with timescales
- resources required.

Action plans should prepare the way forward. How this will work will depend on several factors. Hargreaves and Hopkins (1991, p. 65) identify the activities required to make the plan work:

- sustaining commitment during implementation
- checking the progress of implementation
- overcoming any problems encountered
- checking the success of implementation
- taking stock
- reporting progress
- constructing the next professional development plan.

Development opportunities in school – mentoring

Mentoring is a positive mechanism for developing the skills for leading learning in the classroom to raise the attainment of every child. Through the process, it contributes to the professional development of both the mentor and mentee. The stages of mentoring will involve a period of **induction** for the mentor and mentee. This comprises educating, role modelling, consulting, networking and counselling. During this stage, both mentor and mentee need to ensure that they are the most appropriate people for the role. Interpersonal skills are essential for effective

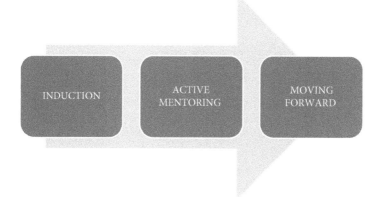

Fig. 14 Stages of mentoring

monitoring. **Active mentoring** will involve further negotiations between mentor and mentee. The framework for the development of the relationship will need to be agreed. Changes may occur as the balance of the relationship moves from dominant/subordinate positions to a relationship with greater equality.

Ultimately the relationship will change to that of a peer/friend. If specific targets have been set, once these have been reached a sense of becoming an equal is readily acknowledged. If the relationship is less ordered there may be difficulty in recognising the true meaning of the process. At no time should a sense of hierarchy dominate the relationship. The stages of mentoring are represented in Figure 14 (above).

These are some possible drawbacks to mentoring. Mentors may pass on bad habits, may not be qualified/able to impart their knowledge of their job, may lack the required patience, may be reluctant to pass on their skills or may be too closely involved to see their job from another person's perspective. However, mentoring is a process whereby you can pass on to someone else your knowledge, understanding, skills and abilities. As a method of developing the knowledge, understanding, skills and abilities of teachers, it has proven qualities.

Developing and leading teams

Effective teams will enable professional development to occur as a matter of course. Staff will feel able to participate. Respect is critical to the process, as is a recognised system of operating as a team. For a team to be effective, members must know their role, know their team and know their managers. The following characteristics of an effective team will help you to reflect on how you might develop a team focused on raising attainment across the school.

Checklist: creating effective teams

Effective teams to raise attainment across the school:

- Have clear objectives and goals – are you asking people to focus on data/ teaching and learning/SEND/Pupil Premium children etc., and is there a time limit?
- Promote openness and non-confrontation, which is dependent on effective communication – you want to hear everyone's point of view. Do you ask them to identify areas where they feel pupil attainment could be raised, why and how, etc.?
- Support and trust – listen and understand the other's point of view. Is there a note taker? Is your team like a 'think tank'; everyone has something to contribute?
- Co-operate – share and develop ideas for raising attainment in a democratic and creative manner.
- Have sound procedures – ENABLE everyone to contribute. Take turns.
- Have appropriate leadership – know and understand your team members, their values and beliefs. How does this contribute to raising children's attainment in the context of your school?
- Regularly review – monitor and evaluate. How much progress is the team making? Do you need to add a new step to bring discussion further?
- Promote individual development – individuals should have the opportunity to develop their strengths in the team.
- Have sound inter-group relations – develop a commitment to teach pupils through openness and trust.

Development through research

The longer-term intention of teachers engaging with research is to encourage deeper reflection on the possibilities of change to improve practice and children's outcomes. Knowing and understanding the research process is the first step to developing a research mind and reflecting on how it can become part of day-to-day practice. An example might be noticing that pupils get better outcomes when they self-evaluate their own learning. This might prompt a teacher to think about introducing it across the class as a means of improving pupil progress and attainment. However, new ways of working can also bring their challenges in terms of time, pupil attitude and school policy. To make the change, it might be better to carry out your own research in the classroom (action research), which gives a greater understanding of how and why it works/does not work and provides an evidence base to share across the school and with a wider audience.

Action research

Action research is acting and researching at the same time, where the emphasis is on the involvement and participation of the researcher/teacher; it is associated with the qualitative field of research. Action research finds its roots in the early work of Kurt Lewin (1946), who developed the simple cyclical process of research as an effective means of bringing about social change. This simple cycle still provides the basic framework for action research within the classroom.

Figure 15 shows the step-by-step process of action research. It is set within a community of practice, because doing action research collaboratively with colleagues is better than one teacher doing it alone. A network of other teacher researchers within the school provides a strong base for discussing issues and academic research articles, planning research together, implementing, monitoring, evaluating and sharing findings.

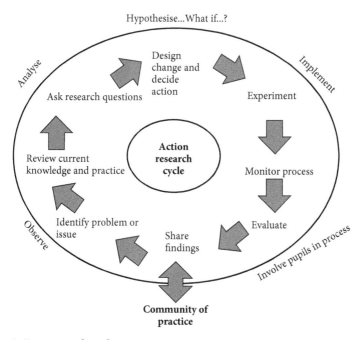

Fig. 15 Action research cycle

(Source: Achievement for All, 2017)

The **observe** phase is when teachers identify a problem or issue, either in classroom practice or professional knowledge (or because it has been identified in the school improvement plan). They decide to find out more about it, by researching other studies or knowledge in the field.

The analyse phase is the planning phase – what research questions will you ask? How will you go about collecting data, etc.? The implement phase is the action – collecting the data – which is followed by collation and analysis of data (on the diagram: involve pupils – because you can ask pupils their opinion on the various aspects of the research in which they participated or their view of the change, and share your findings with them), and the final phase is reflection. Researchers reflect on their findings. Are they what is expected? Were there themes that emerged from the research that had not been anticipated? Shall we repeat the process and make these changes to the action phase?

Bringing about change through action research prompts teachers to engage more fully with policy and the academic evidence base, adding to this through their own research. In so doing, teachers become more confident not only in classroom practice, but also in the development of leadership qualities. In essence, it better enables teachers to lead their own practice and that of others.

Planning and resources

Effective management of staff professional development is a three-part process: plan, act and review, where planning also consists of three elements:

- **Objectives:** goals that are to be achieved in sufficiently detailed and precise terms to enable others to identify whether they have been achieved.
- **Actions:** specification of the activities required to meet the objectives.
- **Resources:** identification of what and who will be required to achieve the objectives and an indication of the time scale.

Planning may involve going around in circles as you consider the various combinations of objectives, actions and resources that will provide you with your way forward. However, this is a necessary process to ensure that all elements are considered. In terms of resources it is worth considering what you have in the school, what you can borrow from other schools, what local authorities provide and/or whether you need to raise funding through grant-making charities. The following are the planning stages for professional development activities:

Objectives	Stage 1	Define the objectives	What are you aiming to achieve?
	Stage 2	Generate and evaluate objectives/actions	What are the courses of action available? Which one will best achieve your objectives?
Actions	Stage 3	Identify the actions	What is required to implement your objectives?
	Stage 4	Sequence the actions	What is the best order?
Resources	Stage 5	Identify the resources	What resources are required?
Review	Stage 6	Review the plan	Will it work? If not return to stages 2 and 3
Preparation	Stage 7	Prepare plans and schedules	Who will do what and when?
Audit	Stage 8	Monitor and evaluate	Re-plan if necessary

Environment scanning

Environment scanning is based on a SWOT analysis: internal strengths and weaknesses and external opportunities and threats. It is used widely by organisations to improve performance. An excellent way to start a staff professional development session focused on raising the attainment of every child is to ask staff to complete a SWOT analysis prior to the session. You can collect, collate and analyse the results, presenting a summary of staff responses at the outset of the session.

Strengths (in raising attainment in the primary classroom)	Weaknesses (in raising attainment in the primary classroom)
Here you can consider strengths (individual and across the school) using the following framework:	Here you can consider weaknesses (individual and across the school) using the following framework:
Leadership Teaching and learning Parent and carer engagement Wider outcomes and opportunities	Leadership Teaching and learning Parent and carer engagement Wider outcomes and opportunities
Opportunities	**Threats**
Consider external opportunities for raising attainment in the primary classroom. You might consider external funding for Pupil Premium children and those with SEND and/or partnerships with teaching schools, independent schools and/or local networks of schools	Consider external issues that may negatively impact on raising the attainment of every child. You might consider school funding, lack of specialist teachers, etc.

For each one, discussion can focus on how the issue is addressed in practice, what each individual teacher can do and how the school can support improvement, moving from good to great.

Developing leadership

Successive government reforms over the past decade have promoted the issue and concept of leadership to the forefront of change within the field of education. Enabling teachers and practitioners to develop and grow as leaders is vital for the development of schools as effective learning communities with good outcomes for all children; leadership and management is one of the key judgements made by Ofsted during inspections. Over recent years distributed leadership has become a widely used model for developing leaders and embedding leadership practice within educational settings. In essence, it involves staff being given ownership of some aspect of their work or their working environment. Evidence shows that when this happens, teachers become more confident leaders of learning in their classroom and children's outcomes are better (Humphrey and Squires, 2011). Professor Alma Harris suggests that:

> Distributed leadership is primarily concerned with the interactions and dynamics of leadership practice rather than a preoccupation with the formal roles and responsibilities traditionally associated with those 'who lead' … It is the practice of leadership that is most important…

> (Harris, 2013, p. vii)

The opportunity to participate in decision-making teams that impact on the effectiveness of an organisation involves participation by team members and delegation from leaders; this supports the development of leadership. Participation, however, can function in the following forms:

- **Consultation:** team members are invited to suggest ideas; decision-making remains the responsibility of the leader.
- **Consent:** team members, as a group, can veto any decision made by the leader.
- **Consensus:** team members are consulted, followed by whole-team involvement in decision-making through majority vote.

The leader of the team should be able to identify which participatory style is applicable to any specific task or situation. Democratic approaches are fine if they suit the task or situation, but equally, autocratic approaches are acceptable and can work in the right circumstances. A leader will need to decide which style to adopt.

Delegation follows different criteria. There are several factors that need to be considered in the process of delegating, which, if implemented appropriately, contribute to the development of effective leaders:

- The quality of the result – will the outcome be good enough?
- The ability of the individual – how capable is the individual of completing the task?

- Relationships – will the individual be coached or left to the task? Either approach could have a positive or negative impact, depending on the context.
- Time – have your staff the time to complete the task or address the issue?
- Ensuring positive aims – delegation should have positive aims, for example, the continuing professional development (CPD) of staff or the most appropriate deployment of staff (which can also contribute to CPD). Do not pass on a job because you find it an unpleasant or time-consuming task.
- Understanding – the delegator should have a clear understanding of both the purpose and process of the task that is delegated
- Proportion – do not abdicate all responsibility for a delegated task, but maintain a fine balance between interest, support and motivation on the one hand and interference or neglect on the other.
- Letting go – this can be difficult. But success has much to do with trust and depends on working things out in a realistic way.
- Communicating – clear and open communication is essential for effective delegation.

Delegation supports the development of leaders and can be supported through training, coaching or mentoring.

Self-evaluation

Professional development sits within the context of improving children's outcomes or raising the attainment of every child, no matter what their challenge, background or need. It is helpful to evaluate your practice in the context of raising achievement. The following questionnaire explores the relationship between process and outcomes and will help you to consider where you are in relation to teaching and learning styles. As you complete it, reflect on your views and consider what/how you could do it better.

Rate the following statements on a 1–5 scale (1= agreement; 5 = disagreement)

1. My job is to get across the facts.
2. What the pupils need to know is in the textbooks and on the worksheets.
3. Essentially, I have to be in control of the classroom.
4. I have to decide on the learning outcomes.
5. It's up to me to decide on whether the pupils have learnt something.

6. I have to be in charge of the resources.
7. The pupils do not need to know the end point; they just have to cope with each step.
8. If the pupils do not learn something, they just need to work harder.
9. There are a lot of material that the class must get through; that is the main task.
10. I must look for the right answers.

Ten takeaway tips for successful CPD

1. Professional development will lead to school improvement.
2. Avoid the tensions that can exist between individual and school requirements (consider how school and staff development should be linked).
3. Target-setting is required if performance review is to be developmental.
4. Action plans are required for professional development activities.
5. Self-development is systematic, beginning with self-evaluation and leading to the identification of available choices and self-development opportunities.
6. Mentoring is a positive mechanism for developing the skills for leading learning in the classroom to raise the attainment of every child; the relationship should not be hierarchical.
7. For a team to be effective, it is essential for members to know their role, know their team and know their managers.
8. All professional development activities should be monitored, evaluated and reviewed.
9. Review should answer the question 'what does professional development bring to a professional career?'
10. A learning culture should be accessible to all members of the school community; this is further developed through teacher engagement with research.

2   Training plans

Overview

What follows is a training pack to help you reflect on how you raise the attainment of all children in your classroom and school. The training plans are based on and developed from Part 1 of this book, which you should reflect on to support delivery of the sessions. They are split into three sections.

1. Twilight sessions

There are 13 one-hour twilight sessions for you to carry out over one or two terms, or they can also be used consecutively as an INSET over two days.

2. 30-minute sessions

There are ten 30-minute sessions for teachers to focus on their own personal and professional development. These help trainees to consider how they can further develop their practice to raise attainment in the classroom and across the school. These can also be used as part of a whole-school INSET.

3. 15-minute sessions

There are eight 15-minute sessions that you could use at various points during the day. These would work well as a series of short breakfast CPD sessions to help teachers focus on their practice and reflect further on how you can better raise attainment in the classroom.

Each training session includes three sections:

- a planning document for the series of sessions
- session step-by-step instructions
- a full set of PowerPoint slides, which can be downloaded.

Planning document

The table provides an overview of everything you need to know about the group of training sessions. Below is an annotated example showing you what goes in each section.

Focus	Notes
Facilitators and audience	*Who is this session for? And who will lead it? This might include a key teacher within the school or an external organisation.*
Topics covered	*A numbered list of the main topics you'll cover in the training session.*
Preparation tasks	*Things that the trainer needs to prepare before the session – e.g. if they'd need to email anything round, do print-outs, read a certain blog or chapter from a book.*
Resources required	*Everything needed for the session: PowerPoint, print out, any technology.*
Preparation time	*In minutes/hours approx.*
Potential problems and solutions	*Problems to keep in mind that you might face within the training session, and how you should deal with them.*
Possible follow-up tasks	*An action point for after the training, for example, trainer could arrange a time to come and visit classrooms to see how it's going.*
Pass it on	*How the idea can be shared throughout the school – e.g. staff could present how it went in a staff meeting.*

Session step-by-step instructions

For each session you are provided with detailed notes on each stage and step-by-step instructions. The guidance given throughout Part 1 of this book will have given you the knowledge you need to give the sessions and Chapter 1 of Part 2 will help you to prepare for the training. The training plans follow a similar structure throughout and suggestions for timings are provided as well as links to the relevant slides for each stage of the session.

PowerPoint slides

There is a PowerPoint presentation provided for every training session, which can be downloaded from the online resources. Further, detailed notes are given on each PowerPoint slide where needed, providing extra advice on running the training.

Before each session

Getting the room right and making everyone welcome is an important aspect of professional development sessions. Before the session ensure that:

- you arrive early (15 minutes)
- you have set up the room as you want it
- the PowerPoint is in place and it works
- you have printed any resources
- if you want a seating plan, have that clearly visible at the entrance.

You may want to have a 'thought' or reflection as the first slide on the PowerPoint. Colleagues can consider this as they are waiting. It is helpful to be welcoming and make the room as welcoming as possible. Everyone is busy and providing a relaxed and calm atmosphere will make a big difference to the session.

Supporting resources

Two copies of the reflection questions at the end of Chapter 5 (p. 85) Part 1 should be given to each participant at the beginning of the CPD sessions. They should reflect on this and complete relevant sections before each CPD session and complete it again in the week after each session. The idea is to self-evaluate the CPD.

Twilight sessions

Planning document

Focus	Notes
Facilitators and audience	This series of twilight sessions is for school leaders, teachers and teaching assistants. You can get help running some of the sessions from the professional development co-ordinator or a key teacher/leader.
Topics covered in the series	1. Building the core 2. The 3As – aspiration, access and achievement 3. Assessment and data tracking 4. Planning 5. Behaviour for learning 6. Leading teaching and learning in the classroom 7. Working with teaching assistants 8. Parent and carer engagement 9. SEND and common sensing the Code of Practice 10. Pupil Premium: closing the gap 11. Monitoring and evaluation 12. Motivating others 13. Developing leadership
Preparation tasks	• Email round the above list to staff. • The reflection questions at the end of Chapter 5, Part 1 are a useful starting point for all CPD as they enable teaching staff/school leaders and teaching assistants to reflect on their own practice before they come to the session. • Provide photocopies of the relevant reflection questions at the end of Chapter 5, Part 1 before the session for staff to reflect on.
Resources required	• PowerPoint • flip chart and pens • A4 paper and pens • you can send round the PowerPoint after each session.

Focus	Notes
Preparation time	• It is suggested that that you go through each PowerPoint before each of the sessions. • Familiarise yourself with the content and use this book to add any extra details you want. Everyone has their own way of preparing and you must spend the time you feel you need. • This may take between 30 and 60 minutes, including 15 minutes to set up the room on the day and gather resources. Printing is not needed.
Potential problems and solutions	Staff may feel they already do a lot to raise attainment through the various areas covered by the individual session titles. They may do, but when you focus on your practice you realise there is always more to do; there are gaps. What someone thought was great practice can overlook taking practice to the next level. The idea is to keep getting better – going from good to great. If time is taken to prepare the session and consideration given to the reflections/activities, there should be no problems in delivery and enabling staff to consider culture, change and staff leading change.
Possible follow-up tasks	• The reflection activities that are done during the session are designed so that participants can 'take that away' and reflect on it further. These sessions are focused on developing individual practice in the context of whole-school improvement. • It is suggested that the CPD should be accompanied by short lesson observations (peer). • Re-visit the relevant reflection questions at the end of Chapter 5, Part 1 in the week following the individual session.
Pass it on	There are a number of options for 'passing it on'. These include: • Staff giving feedback in a meeting about some aspect of their practice they changed as a result of the sessions and how that raised the attainment of pupils (or certain pupils). • Staff can implement meetings to discuss progress of pupils (data-led meetings). • Staff can develop a research group to develop practice through their own research or develop evidence-based practice.

Session step-by-step instructions
Session 1: Building the core

PowerPoint: Twilight session 1_Building the core

Focus	Timings	Format	Content
Intro	10 minutes	Presentation	Introduce the topic of 'Building the core' to the attendees: Slides 1–5 • Define 'the core'. Slides 6–7 • Focus on why schools need to build the core in all children. Slides 9–10 • Focus on equity in education and what equity in education means short and long term.

Activity 1	10 minutes discussion
	
	3 minutes feedback
		Group discussion	• Split attendees into groups of 3–4 and display Slide 11, which considers a whole-school approach to 'building the core'.
			• Ask them to look across leadership, teaching and learning, parent and carer engagement and wider opportunities and consider:
			  - What is the current practice in building the core in children in these areas?
			  - Are there any gaps?

		Whole-group discussion	• Feed back to the main group.
Presentation	3 minutes	Presentation	Talk the attendees through Slides 12–15. • Define what is meant by school culture.
Activity 2	10 minutes discussion 3 minutes feedback	Group discussion	• Ask attendees to resume their groups of 4 and display Slide 16: *How would you respond to the following challenges?* - *a lack of aspiration amongst teaching staff across the school for pupil outcomes* - *a high proportion of pupils who cannot overcome barriers to learning* - *a lack of parent and carer engagement in the school.* • Ask attendees to discuss these issues in their groups, in the context of culture, attitudes and what needs to change to bring about improvement.
		Whole-group discussion	• Feed back to the group.

Focus	Timings	Format	Content
Conclusion	4 minutes	Presentation	Talk the attendees through Slides 17–20. Slides 17–19 • Consider 'vision' and how sharing a common vision across the school supports development of culture across the school. Slide 20 • This brings the session to a close and reflects on what an inclusive approach to leadership means.
Final reflection/ takeaway activity	10 minutes discussion 3 minutes feedback	Group reflection and takeaway activity	Finish the session by displaying Slide 21 and, in their groups, ask attendees to consider the common questions with 'new' thinking. • They should reflect on what they have covered in the session and think about the types of responses they would now give. • This can be started in the session or it can be a 'takeaway' activity' for participants to reflect on. • Reflections should be made in the context of creating the 'right' culture and their attitudes and how this influences what happens in the classroom.
		Whole-group discussion	• Feed back to the group.
Closing questions	4 minutes	Questions	At the end, spend 4 minutes closing the session and taking any questions.

Session 2: Aspiration, access and achievement: the 3As

PowerPoint: Twilight session 2_Aspiration, access and achievement

Focus	Timings	Format	Content

Presentation	11 minutes (1 minute per slide)	**Presentation**	Introduce the topic of 'Aspiration, access and achievement: the 3As' to the attendees:
			Slides 1–4
			• Give a general introduction to aspiration, access and achievement.
			Slides 5–11
			• Define aspiration.
			• Next, focus on the different elements of aspiration, giving simple case studies of how schools have gone about increasing aspiration across the school. The elements are:
			  - attitudes
			  - confidence
			  - parental engagement
			  - motivation
			  - teacher aspirations.

Activity 1	10 minutes discussion 3 minutes feedback	**Individual reflection** **Group discussion**	Slide 12 Ask attendees to reflect on the first part of the session individually: • Reflect on all the ways you show children that you have high aspirations for them. Then, in groups of 2–3, ask them to discuss what they currently do and then decide: • How could you do this better?

Presentation	6 minutes (1 minute per slide)		Slides 13–18
			• Define access.
			• Focus on access and enabling all children to access learning. Share simple case studies to show what this means in practice, focusing on the following areas:
			  - behaviour
			  - participation in wider school
			  - developing positive relationships with others
			  - attendance.

Activity 2	10 minutes discussion 3 minutes feedback	**Individual reflection** **Group discussion**	Slide 19 Ask attendees to reflect on what they've learnt about access to learning individually: • Consider what practices you currently use to support access to the curriculum and wider school activities for all children. Then, in groups of 2–3, ask them to discuss what they currently do and then decide: • How could you do this better?

Focus	Timings	Format	Content
Presentation	2 minutes	Presentation	Slide 20 • Discuss what is meant by achievement and what it means in practice.

Activity 3	10 minutes discussion
	
	3 minutes feedback
		Group discussion and takeaway activity	Slide 21
			Ask attendees, in their groups, to discuss achievement and their current practices that contribute to raising achievement.
			• Consider the extent to which you do the following and how you could do them better:
			  - Monitor pupil progress against targets.
			  - Put interventions in place only when needed.
			  - Have pupil progress meetings.
			  - Encourage pupils to take responsibility for their progress.
			  - Outline next steps in learning for pupils.
			  - Develop attendance initiatives.
			  - Organise workshops for parents to develop their role in supporting children's reading and maths at home.
			  - Use pupil data to measure progress and inform planning.
			  - Work effectively with teaching assistants to improve pupil achievement.

Closing questions	2 minutes	Questions	At the end, spend 2 minutes closing the session and taking any questions.

Session 3: Assessment and data tracking

PowerPoint: Twilight session 3_Assessment and data tracking

Focus	Timings	Format	Content
Introduction	15 minutes	**Presentation**	Introduce the topic with Slides 1–8. • Refer briefly back to the previous two sessions, reminding the attendees about the challenge of underachievement and the 3As. • Introduce assessment and data. • The idea is to reflect on each slide. In many ways, the content is probably familiar, but it is about reflecting on it and thinking how you do it and how you might do it better.
Activity 1	10 minutes discussion 5 minutes feedback	**Group discussion**	Slide 9 gets attendees to really focus on assessment and data recording. In groups of 2–3, ask them to reflect on: • How good are your current tracking systems? • How could you do it better? • There are prompts on Slide 9 for them to use as discussion points.
		Whole-group feedback	Feed back as a whole group. • The feedback gives time for collective thoughts and possible consideration of best practice. • Record feedback on a flip chart.
Presentation	3 minutes (1 minute on each slide)	**Presentation**	Slides 10–12 • Reflect on what each slide is stating as you present it. • As in the first part of the session, the idea is for attendees to consider their current practice so that when they come to the following reflection they will have extra ideas to talk about.
Activity 2	10 minutes discussion 3 minutes feedback	**Group discussion**	Slide 13 gets attendees to really focus on data. In groups of 2–3, ask them to reflect on: • How do you turn 'raw' assessment data into meaningful data that tells you something about pupil learning? • Do you clearly record the impact of any intervention and consider whether it needs to be changed/adapted? • Do you clearly record any changes you make to the curricula to improve children's learning? (Can you see this at a glance?)
		Whole-group feedback	Feed back as a whole group. • The feedback gives time for collective thoughts and possible consideration of best practice. • Record feedback on a flip chart.

Focus	Timings	Format	Content
Conclusion	3 minutes presentation 10 minutes discussion	Presentation Whole-group discussion	Summarise the session. • Reflect on each point in Slide 14. • Finish by discussing the outcomes of the two discussions (recorded on the flip chart). • Consider what should be taken forward and developed as 'best practice'.
Closing questions	1 minute	Questions	At the end, spend 1 minute closing the session and taking any questions.

Session 4: Planning

PowerPoint: Twilight session 4_planning

Focus	Timings	Format	Content
Introduction	7 minutes (1 minute per slide)	Presentation	Introduce the topic with Slides 1–7. • What is planning? • What is successful planning? • Introduce long-term planning.
Activity 1	7 minutes discussion	Group discussion	Slide 8 Ask attendees to work in groups of 2–3 to reflect on long-term planning.
	2 minutes feedback		• Different elements of long-term planning are listed on the slide: - How could you better implement each of them in your long-term planning?
		Whole-group feedback	Feed back to the group
Presentation	3 minutes (1 minute per slide)	Presentation	Slides 9–11 • Introduce medium-term planning. • Introduce short-term planning.
Activity 2	7 minutes discussion	Group discussion	Slide 12 Ask attendees to work in their groups again.

	2 minutes feedback		• Consider how your views and attitudes influence what happens in the classroom – even at the planning stages:
			  - How do my beliefs, values and attitude affect what and how I teach?
			  - Am I in danger of planning lessons based on my own preferences and experiences rather than the children's needs?
			  - Do I have high expectations of the children I teach?
			  - How have recent experiences caused me to alter/develop these beliefs, values and attitudes and adapt my practice?

		Whole-group feedback	Feed back as a whole group. Slide 13 can be used if there is time or can be taken away to work on.

Activity 3	7 minutes discussion	Group discussion	Back in their groups, ask attendees to reflect on the learning environment.
			• Display Slide 14. The learning environment can be given less attention at the planning stage.
			• Ask attendees to consider:
			  - How will I arrange the environment to encourage maximum scope for enquiry, problem-solving and creativity to take place?
			  - Am I making the best use of the other adults working with me?
			  - Are there constraints in terms of the physical space?

	2 minutes feedback		
		Whole-group feedback	Feed back as a whole group.

Focus	Timings	Format	Content
Activity 4	7 minutes discussion 2 minutes feedback	**Group discussion**	Attendees to continue working in their groups. • Slide 15 is a reflection on children's learning outcomes and how planning needs to have a certain element of 'working back' from the intended learning outcomes. The idea is to consider ALL children. • Ask attendees to consider: - What can be observed? - What can be assessed? - What will the children learn and how will they show what they have learnt? - Do I provide children with opportunity for peer assessment, metacognition (knowledge of how they are learning), reflection and time to talk about their learning, the process and the outcomes?
		Whole-group feedback	Feed back as a whole group.
Presentation	2 minutes	**Presentation**	Slide 16 focuses on the lesson plan and how long-, medium- and short-term plans are brought together in a lesson plan.
Conclusion and takeaway	7 minutes discussion 2 minutes feedback	**Presentation**	Ask attendees to work on their groups for this last reflection. • Slide 17 is a group discussion focusing on effective and successful planning – at each stage – to ensure that teaching and learning is always focused on getting the best outcomes for each child. • Ask them to analyse and evaluate their current practice. Feed back.
Closing questions	3 minutes	**Questions**	At the end, spend 3 minutes closing the session and taking any questions.

Session 5: Behaviour For learning

PowerPoint: Twilight session 5_Behaviour for learning

Focus	Timings	Format	Content
Introduction	10 minutes (1 minute per slide)	Presentation	Introduce behaviour for learning using Slides 1–10. • Talk through the basics: - The common behaviour features in effective schools. - How it's important to communicate high expectations to students. - The importance of responsive instruction and its features. - The importance of developing and reinforcing positive dispositions for learning. - The qualities of an independent learner. - The qualities of mastery-oriented learners.
Activity 1	15 minutes discussion 5 minutes feedback	Group discussion	Ask attendees to work in groups of 2–3 to consider what's been discussed so far. • Slide 11 focuses on developing children as independent learners. • Ask attendees to consider their current practice. • How do they develop the qualities of independent learning in their students? • How can they do it better? • Consideration should be given to ALL children.
		Whole-group feedback	Feed back to the group.
Presentation	3 minutes (1 minute per slide)	Presentation	Slides 12–14 • Present the research and the recommendations for what works best in reducing classroom behaviour problems. • Talk through the recommendations in practice.
Activity 2	18 minutes	Group discussion	Ask attendees to work in their groups again. • Slides 15 and 16 go together and the idea is to start developing a whole-school approach to good behaviour for learning. • In their groups they should answer the questions displayed and start to work on ideas for whole-school approaches to improving behaviour.
	5 minutes	Whole-group feedback	Feed back to the group.
Summary	1 minute	Presentation	Summarise what's been covered in the session. • Slide 17 is a simple summary of what is needed for good behaviour for learning.
Conclusion and closing questions	3 minutes	Questions and summary	Spend 3 minutes at the end summing up and answering any questions.

Session 6: Leading teaching and learning

PowerPoint: Twilight session 6_Leading teaching and learning

Focus	Timings	Format	Content

Introduction	3 minutes	Presentation	Introduce the session.
			
			• Slides 1–5 are meant to encourage and promote thought on what *is* a great teacher:
			  - Is it something more than their knowledge and pedagogy?
			  - And how do they develop those particular characteristics?

Activity 1	3 minutes brainstorming 2 minutes feedback	**Individual brainstorming** **Whole-group feedback**	Working individually, ask attendees to consider the question on Slide 6: • What are the characteristics of a great teacher? • They should use the information from the first part of session as well as their own ideas. Feed back ideas to the whole group.
Presentation	6 minutes (1 minute per slide)	Presentation	Slides 7–12 focus on the particular techniques and practices of good teaching and learning in the classroom. • The idea is to present each slide, reflecting on how it is done in practice.

Activity 2	8 minutes discussion
	
	3 minutes feedback
		Group discussion
		
		Whole-group feedback
			Slide 13 follows on from the topics presented in the previous 6 slides. Ask attendees to work in groups of 2–3.
			
			• Reflect on the following: How do you:
			  - Question children to advance their learning?
			  - Prompt children to advance their learning?
			  - Praise children to advance their learning?
			
			Feed back as a whole group.
			
			• Record some of the comments on the flip chart, with a view to developing a bank of questions/prompts and praise to be used across the school.

Presentation	2 minutes (1 minute per slide)	Presentation	Slides 14–15 discuss closing the attainment gap. • The idea is to present each slide, reflecting on how it is done in practice.

Focus	Timings	Format	Content
Activity 3	15 minutes discussion 10 minutes feedback	Group discussion	Slides 16–17 Ask attendees to work in their groups again. • Reflect on the elements of individualised learning. - How many do you use in your current practice? - How could you improve your current practice?
		Whole-group feedback	Feed back as a group. • Bring the group's thoughts together, recording ideas on the flip chart.
Activity 4	5 minutes discussion 2 minutes feedback	Group discussion	Bring the session to a close by asking attendees the question on Slide 18: • What strategies do you use to ensure that all children develop confidence in their competencies? • This is an end-of-session activity focusing on how teachers, through their teaching and pedagogy, give children confidence in their knowledge, skills and understanding. • Display the flip chart with the ideas listed throughout the session and ask attendees to consider these ideas and their own to discuss this final question.
		Whole-group feedback	Feed back as a group.
Conclusion and closing questions	1 minute	Questions and summary	Spend 1 minute at the end summing up and answering any questions.

Session 7: Working with teaching assistants

PowerPoint: Twilight session 7_Working with teaching assistants

Focus	Timings	Format	Content
Introduction	3 minutes	Presentation	Introduce the session using Slides 1–2. • The intention of this session is to reflect on how teachers work with teaching assistants and how they could do it better. • The focus is always getting the best outcomes for children and helping them to make good progress. • Teaching assistants should be able to work with you to support that process. • Use Slide 2 to consider whether there is an inclusive approach to TAs across your school. • This is important in developing their role and helping them to better support and develop children's learning.

Activity 1	10 minutes discussion
	
	5 minutes feedback
		Group discussion	Ask attendees to work in groups and display Slide 3.
			• The idea is to consider how teachers work with TAs.
			• Teachers should be doing all of the practices listed in Slide 3 in their work with TAs.
			• Ask attendees:
			  - To reflect on whether and how they do them.
			  - How could they do them better?
			• Also, reflect back on Slide 2: if all these practices are in place, then it will be easier and more effective for teachers to work with TAs.

		Whole-group feedback	Feed back as a group. • Record ideas on a flip chart.

Activity 2	20 minutes discussion
	
	8 minutes feedback
		Group discussion	Ask attendees to continue working in their groups and display Slides 4 and 5.
			• Consider your current practice with teaching assistants.
			• Consider how it could be better.
			  - Do your teaching assistants know and understand their role and purpose in the context of the teacher?
			  - Do you encourage TAs to have an aspirational attitude, communicated with the pupils with whom they work?
			  - Do TAs know and understand their role in the context of increasing pupil progress and attainment?
			  - Do TAs know: the pupils with whom they work, the relevant subject knowledge and National Curriculum, the expected outcomes of what they are teaching, how to question pupils to develop their learning and how to assess pupils?

		Whole-group feedback	Feed back as a group. • Record the feedback on the flipchart.

Focus	Timings	Format	Content
Activity 3	13 minutes	Whole-group discussion	In the final part of the session, bring the group together. • Look at comments from both reflections listed on the flip chart. • Consider how practice and working with teaching assistants (across the school) could be better. • The aim is to raise the achievement of each child.
Closing questions	1 minute	Questions	At the end, spend 1 minute closing the session and taking any questions.

Session 8: Parent and carer engagement

PowerPoint: Twilight session 8_Parent and carer engagement

Focus	Timings	Format	Content
Introduction	7 minutes	Presentation	This session is slightly different to the other sessions within this group as its focus is to develop a whole-school approach to parent and carer engagement by the end of the session. Introduce parent and carer engagement using slides 1–7. • What is it? • Why is it needed? • The importance of parents engaging with their child's learning (not necessarily with the school, although that is relevant). • Thoughts should revolve around development of workshops/support for development of the home learning environment/engagement though online, etc. Supplement with details on parent and carer engagement from Part 1.

Activity 1	25 minutes
	
	 10 minutes feedback
		Group discussion	Ask attendees to work in groups of 2–3 and display Slides 8–9.
			
			 • Ask them to reflect on and discuss their current parental engagement:
			    - How well do I know the parents and carers of the children in my class?
			    - How effectively do I communicate with parents and carers? (In what way?)
			    - Is there a shared understanding of how their child should behave, and about attendance?
			    - Is the home situation stable or changing? (How can I support parents and carers to better support learning at home?)
			    - How well do I know the family?
			    - How do I support parents in developing the home learning environment?

		Whole-group feedback	Feed back as a whole class. • Record ideas on the flipchart.
Activity 2 and takeaway	15 minutes	Group discussion	In the final part of the session, ask attendees to work in their groups to develop a whole-school approach to parent and carer engagement. • Consider those who never engage with the school and how you will enable them to do that. • What outcomes do you expect? • Display the ideas on the flipchart to help guide the discussion and planning.
Closing questions	3 minutes	Questions	At the end, spend 3 minutes closing the session and taking any questions.

Session 9: Common sensing the Code of Practice

• Ask school SENCO to contribute to this session.

PowerPoint: Twilight session 9_Common sensing the Code of Practice

Focus	Timings	Format	Content

Introduction	5 minutes	Presentation	Introduce the topic of common sensing the Code of Practice.
			• Slides 1–9 are presentations focusing on SEND in practice in the classroom and rooted in the Code of Practice. They cover:
			  - A presentation of the challenges.
			  - The importance of knowing the pupils.
			  - The importance of being able to define SEN and SEN provision.
			  - The principles of an inclusive leadership model.

Activity 1	1 minute	Individual reflection	Display Slide 10 and ask attendees to reflect individually on how much they know, and how much they rely on their SENCO. • Have all the staff read the 0–25 SEN Code of Practice? • Are all staff clear about their statutory duties in the new Code of Practice? • Do all staff know what they look like in practice? • Do all staff know how to use the Code of Practice for day-to-day teaching and learning to maximise pupil outcomes (e.g. what, when, where and how)? This is for teachers to reflect on how much they know and how much they rely on the SENCO. Don't have a feedback session – let teachers reflect quietly on this.
Presentation	5 minutes	Presentation	Slides 11–17 • Present the graduated response using Slides 11–14. • For the next part of the presentation, it may be helpful to ask the school SENCO to contribute. • Present Slides 15–17, reflecting on what it looks like in practice.
Activity 2	15 minutes discussion 8 minutes feedback	Group discussion	Display Slide 18 and ask attendees to work in groups of 2–3. • Ask the SENCO to facilitate a discussion session around the graduated response. Feed back to the group. Record feedback on the flip chart.

Focus	Timings	Format	Content
Presentation	3 minutes	Presentation	Present Slides 19–21. • It is important to consider: - Are all teachers doing what is expected of them?
Activity 3	12 minutes discussion 5 minutes feedback	Group discussion	Ask attendees to work in their groups again and display Slide 22. They should consider how they would respond to the following: • Have you evaluated your practice against your SEN Information Report? • Have you engaged parents and carers in their children's learning and given them a 'voice' in what happens in school? • Do you have a system for the clear and accurate identification of pupils with SEN and are you applying the graduated approach effectively? • How closely do you monitor pupil data? • Do you use the Code of Practice for day-to-day teaching and learning to maximise pupil outcomes (e.g. what, when, where and how)? • What systems are in place to ensure that children and young people are involved in all aspects of school life? Feed back as a group. • Record comments on the flip chart and reflect on how the comments could be used to improve practice across the school.
Conclusion and takeaway	6 minutes	Questions	At the end, answer questions and consider whether further development in this area is needed (for the school).

Session 10: Pupil Premium: closing the gap

PowerPoint: Twilight session 10_Pupil premium

Focus	Timings	Format	Content
Introduction	13 minutes	Presentation	The aim of this session is to focus on developing best practice in supporting and developing Pupil Premium pupils.
			Introduce the topic of Pupil Premium.
			• Slides 1–13 should be reflected upon as you present them. Don't spend too long on each, but the idea is to enable teachers to reflect on their current practice. Discuss:
			- The link between academic underperformance and socio-economic disadvantage.
			- SEN and links with poverty.
			- The difference schools make to social mobility.
			- Literacy and social mobility.
			- Maths and social mobility.
			- Introduction to Pupil Premium and closing the attainment gap.
			- Children's mental health and wellbeing.
			- The best way to spend Pupil Premium funding.
Activity 1	20 minutes discussion 10 minutes feedback	Group discussion	Slides 14 and 15 are aimed at exploring current practice in relation to Pupil Premium pupils and how this can be even better. Attendees should consider:
			- pupils with additional learning needs
			- pupils who are gifted and talented
			- those who may be middle attainers.
			Display Slide 14, which lists ways of effectively using Pupil Premium. For each of the points made on the slide, consider:
			- How you would respond.
			- How you do it in practice.
			- What are the gaps in practice?
			- How could you do it better?
		Whole-group feedback	Feed back as a group.

Focus	Timings	Format	Content
Activity 2	5 minutes discussion	**Group discussion**	Display Slide 15 and ask attendees to discuss and answer the questions. • What educational offer does each pupil receive? • How is provision strategically planned and implemented? • How are funds allocated to the most vulnerable pupils? • How is activity and impact monitored, recorded and reviewed? • What financial monitoring and reporting is in place? • How is progress accelerated for the most vulnerable pupils using the Pupil Premium grant?
	5 minutes feedback		
		Whole-group feedback	Feed back as a group.
Activity 3	1 minute	**Whole-group discussion**	Bring the session together by displaying Slide 16, which includes 'Spending the Pupil Premium wisely: 10 point plan by Dunford'. • Ask individuals to comment and reflect.
Conclusion and takeaway	6 minutes	**Questions**	Spend the final minutes of the session bringing together points/ideas/challenges that could be further developed in the school to improve practice around Pupil Premium pupils.

Session 11: Monitoring and evaluation

PowerPoint: Twilight session 11_Monitoring and evaluation

Focus	Timings	Format	Content
Introduction and presentation	26 minutes	Presentation	Slide 1
			You can provide the usual introduction, along with the following:
			This session provides a general session on monitoring and evaluation.
			The process can be used for monitoring and evaluating:
			- teaching practices
			- interventions
			- pupil learning.
			Slides 2–27
			Ensure participants are clear what each means. Present the slides to them, including:
			• Why there is a need for monitoring.
			• Basics of effective monitoring.
			• A framework for monitoring.
			• Measuring success.
			• Monitoring in practice.
			• A checklist for schools.
			• What is evaluation?
			• Evaluation in contrast to monitoring.
			• Evaluation and teacher development.
			• The purpose of evaluating plans.
			• A checklist for planning and evaluation.
Activity 1	20 minutes discussion 10 minutes feedback	Practical	Display Slide 28.
			The second half of the session is practical.
			• Each attendee will need a piece of A4 paper and a pen.
			• Ask attendees to form groups of 3–4.
			• In group discussion they will come up with an evaluation plan for the following scenario:
			You decide to introduce a 'fun with numbers' session as a lunchtime club one day a week open to all children. The aim is to improve outcomes in maths, help children enjoy maths and help children to develop a 'can do' attitude to maths.
			• *How would you go about evaluating the impact of the club?*
			• *(Consider what you need to 'measure' and how you would measure it.)*

Focus	Timings	Format	Content

			Tell attendees it often helps to plan back from the 3 aims.
			• They need to think:
			  - Who?
			  - How?
			  - Where?
			  - What?
			Get each group to feed back their plan to the whole group.

Closing questions	4 minutes	**Questions**	In the final 4 minutes, close the session and answer any questions.

These last two sessions are aimed at teachers developing their own practice and both look towards developing leadership qualities and practice. It is important for teachers to consider their own development and career progression, but equally in the context of raising attainment in the classroom.

Session 12: Motivating others

PowerPoint: Twilight session 12_Motivating others

Focus	Timings	Format	Content
Pre-intro reflection activity	5 minutes reflection	**Individual reflection**	Slide 1 Introduction Slide 2 Start the session with a short reflection exercise. Ask attendees to work individually. • The scenario is: *A member of your team is demotivated. What would you consider and/or implement to enhance their motivation?* • The idea is to reflect, at a more personal level, on: - what motivates you - what motivates others. • There will be strong similarities because basic human characteristics are common to all.
	2 minutes feedback		
		Whole-group feedback	Feed back ideas as a group. Display Slide 3, which provides a general summary of what to consider in motivating your team.
Introduction	5 minutes	**Presentation**	Slides 4–6 • Present the 3 models: - the social model - the rational-economic model - the self-actualising model. • After each slide, ask attendees the extent to which they agree/disagree with each model. • Do all models need to be combined?
Activity 1	5 minutes discussion	**Group discussion**	Ask attendees to form groups of 2–3 and display Slide 7. • Groups are to reflect on the 3 models and the extent to which they can be considered on a standalone basis or otherwise. - To what extent are these models useful for practice? - Is there any one model that best describes reasons for your motivation? - To what extent do you think people act within one of the 3 models? To what extent do you think people's reasons for motivation lie within parts of the 3 models? - In the context of the school (from the leaders' and teachers' point of view) what are the advantages and disadvantages of each model?
	3 minutes feedback		
		Whole-group feedback	Feed back to the whole group.

Focus	Timings	Format	Content
Presentation	8 minutes	**Presentation**	Present Maslow's hierarchy of needs using Slides 8–11. • Reflect on each one as you present. Display Slide 12. This is a summary, bringing the theory of the previous slides into a practical focus. Present the content in Slides 13–15, which focus on: • Delegation of tasks. • How you can get the best results from people through effective delegation. • How this relates to motivation – often by giving people more individual responsibility.
Activity 2	15 minutes discussion 5 minutes feedback	**Group discussion**	Ask attendees to form their groups again and display Slide 16. • How would you manage delegation of tasks? • Delegation of tasks reduces my workload. Discuss. Encourage the attendees to focus their discussion on: • Delegation of tasks.
		Whole-group discussion	• How this can be motivational. Feed back ideas to the whole group.
Conclusion and takeaway activity	12 minutes	**Group reflection**	Bring the discussion together at the end to consider what are the key qualities needed to motivate people: • Teachers/TAs (in particular). • How could this be further developed across the school, particularly in the context of teacher career progression?

Session 13: Developing leadership

PowerPoint: Twilight session 13_Developing leadership

Focus	Timings	Format	Content
Introduction	10 minutes	Presentation	Introduce the topic of developing leadership. • Slides 1–13 are aimed at focusing teachers on developing their own leadership. • It is good to reflect on each slide as you present, enabling teachers to think about their own leadership qualities and how they can be further developed.
Activity 1	10 minutes discussion 10 minutes feedback	Group discussion	Ask attendees to form groups of 2–3 and display Slide 14. They should reflect on the question: • What does middle leadership mean for you? - Reflect on the key characteristics of effective middle leadership. • What characteristics do you think are needed for effective middle leadership?
		Whole-group feedback	Feed back as a whole group. • Record the answers on a flipchart.
Presentation	3 minutes	Presentation	Present Slides 15–20. • Again, present them so that teachers can reflect on their own practice as you go along.
Activity 2	10 minutes discussion 10 minutes feedback	Group discussion	Ask attendees to work in their groups again and show Slide 21. • What does managing change mean to you? - How might you – as a middle leader – develop a positive attitude to change amongst your staff members? - What would you do at the outset to avoid a negative outcome? Feed back as a whole group. • Record the answers on a flipchart.
Conclusion and takeaway activity	6 minutes	Whole-group feedback and discussion	Spend the last 5 – 6 minutes bringing together the key characteristics of effective leadership. • Display the notes you've collected on the flipchart. • Ask attendees how they feel they could develop the list further. • Finally, as a group, develop a list of effective characteristics of leadership.
Closing questions	1 minute	Questions	In the final 1 minute, close the session and answer any questions.

30-minute sessions

Planning document

Focus	Notes
Facilitators and audience	This series of 30-minute sessions is for school leaders, teachers and teaching assistants. You can get help running the sessions from the professional development co-ordinator or a key teacher/leader.
Topics covered	1. Working in teams 2. Developing yourself 3. Engaging with research 4. Creating an enabling learning environment that creates learning for all 5. Wider outcomes and opportunities 6. Case study 1: Parent and carer engagement 7. Case study 2: Tracking progress in maths 8. Case study 3: SEND, differentiation and interventions 9. Case study 4: Quality first teaching 10. Case study 5: Maths using the mastery approach
Preparation tasks	• Email round the above list to staff. • The reflection questions at the end of Chapter 5, Part 1 are a useful starting point for all CPD as they enable teaching staff/school leaders and teaching assistants to reflect on their own practice before they come to the session. • Provide photocopies of the relevant questions from Chapter 5, Part 1 before the session for staff to reflect on.
Resources required	You will need • PowerPoint sildes • flipchart and pens • A4 paper and pens for attendees. • For Session 3, Engaging with research, the session will be easier for attendees if they have had a chance to reflect on a published research report before the session. You can select a report from the completed projects on the EEF website and send the link to attendees. Completed project reports can be found at: https://educationendowmentfoundation.org.uk/projects-and-evaluation/reports/. Ask attendees to reflect on the questions on Slide 19 before the session. You can send round the PowerPoint after each session.
Preparation time	• Go through each PowerPoint before the session. • Familiarise yourself with it and use this book to add any extra details you want. Everyone has their own way of preparing and you must spend the time you feel you need. • This may take between 30 and 60 minutes, including 15 minutes to set up the room on the day and gather resources. • Printing is not needed.

Focus	Notes
Potential problems and solutions	Staff may feel they already do a lot to raise attainment through the various areas covered by the individual session titles. They may do, but when you focus on your practice you realise there is always more to do; there are gaps. And what we thought was great practice can overlook taking practice to the next level. The idea is to keep getting better – going from good to great.
	If time is taken to prepare the session and consideration given to the reflections/activities, there should be no problems in delivery and enabling staff to consider culture, change and staff leading change.
Possible follow-up tasks	• The reflection activities that are done during the session are designed so that participants can 'take that away' and reflect on it further.
	• These sessions are focused on developing individual practice in the context of whole-school improvement. It is suggested that the CPD should be accompanied by short lesson observations (peer).
	• Staff should re-visit the reflection questions in Chapter 5, Part 1 and complete the relevant section in the week following the individual session.
Pass it on	There are a number of options for 'passing it on'. These include staff giving feedback in a meeting about some aspect of their practice they changed as a result of the sessions and how that raised the attainment of pupils (or certain pupils). Staff can implement meetings to discuss progress of pupils (data-led meetings). Staff can develop a research group to develop practice through their own research or develop evidence-based practice.

Session step-by-step instructions

Session 1: Working in teams

PowerPoint: 30min session 1_Working in teams

Focus	Timings	Format	Content
Introduction	5 minutes	Presentation	The aim is to develop team practice and focus on developing and sustaining effective teams. • Slides 1–7 should be presented as they stand, with teachers reflecting on teams as they view the slides.
Activity 1	7 minutes discussion 3 minutes feedback	Group discussion	Ask attendees to get into groups of 2–3 and display Slide 8. • Activity: How would you develop an effective team? *For each of the following consider* *(a) what they mean to you and* *(b) how would you develop them in practice?* - *clear elevating goals* - *results-driven structure* - *competent team members* - *unified commitment* - *collaborative climate* - *standards of excellence* - *external support and recognition* - *effective leadership.* *Discuss in their groups and write down answers*
		Whole-group discussion	Feed back as a group. • Collate answers on the flipchart.
Presentation	2 minutes	Presentation	Present Slides 9–14. • The focus is on effective leadership of teams.
Activity 2	7 minutes discussion 3 minutes feedback	Group discussion	Ask attendees to work in their groups again and display Slide 15. • *Activity: Building effective teams.* - *What strategies do you use to communicate objectives and tasks and unite others in working towards shared goals?* - *How could you do this better?*
		Whole-group discussion	Feed back as a group. • Collate answers on the flipchart.
Conclusion and takeaway	3 minutes	Questions and summary	Spend the last 3 minutes answering questions and summarising. • Bring the session together with a summary of effective team skills. • Display all of the notes you collated on the flipchart.

Session 2: Developing yourself

PowerPoint: 30min session 2_Developing yourself

Focus	Timings	Format	Content
Introduction	5 minutes	Presentation	The aim of this session is to focus on developing yourself as a teacher and a future leader. • The focus is raising attainment in the classroom and how self-development should be centred on that. • Present Slides 1–3.

Activity 1	7 minutes discussion
	
	3 minutes feedback
		Group discussion	Ask attendees to get into groups of 2–3 and display Slide 4.
			• Activity: Career planning key questions:
			  - *What do I value?*
			  - *What is my present situation?*
			  - *Where would I like my career to lead?*
			  - *How might I get there?*
			  - *What help is available?*
			• Activity: Personal qualities needed:
			  - *ability to self-manage*
			  - *clear personal values*
			  - *clear personal objectives*
			  - *an emphasis on continuing personal growth*
			  - *effective problem-solving skills*
			  - *the capacity to be creative and innovative.*

		Whole-group discussion	Feed back as a group.
Presentation	3 minutes	Presentation	Present Slides 5–17. They cover: • How to identify your personal training needs. • In-house staff development activities. • The key features of mentoring.
Activity 2	7 minutes discussion 3 minutes feedback	Group discussion	Ask attendees to work in their groups again and display Slide 18. • Activity: creating a mentoring scheme - *How would you create a mentoring scheme in your department/school?*
		Whole-group discussion	Feed back as a group.
Conclusion and takeaway	2 minutes	Questions and summary	Display Slide 19. • The teacher's self-evaluation is a group discussion and a takeaway activity for attendees to work on in their own time.

Session 3: Engaging with research

PowerPoint: 30min session 3_Engaging with research

Focus	Timings	Format	Content

Introduction and presentation	18 minutes	Presentation	This session is about developing research.
			• Present Slides 1–20. Reflect on each slide as you present it, considering what it means in practice.
			• Topics include:
			  - What are the benefits of research-led practice?
			  - What does it look like in practice?
			  - Doing your own research.

Activity 1	7 minutes discussion
	
	3 minutes feedback
		Group discussion	End the session by bringing together the key points about evaluating research evidence. Attendees will have reflected on the research report you sent prior to the session, along with the questions displayed on Slide 19 and below.
			• Ask attendees to work in groups of 2–3.
			• Display Slide 19:
			  - *Evaluating documents and research.*
			  - *What are their assumptions? (On what have they based their rationale?)*
			  - *Have they stated their assumptions? (You might have to look for them.)*
			  - *Does the evidence support their assumptions?*
			  - *What are the aims/objectives of the research/article?*
			  - *Do you agree with their method – how have they done it/would you do it differently? (bias, no control)*
			  - *Findings – what are they?*
			  - *Any weaknesses?*

		Whole-group discussion	Feed back as a group.
Conclusion and takeaway	2 minutes	Questions and summary	Spend the last 2 minutes answering questions.

Session 4: Creating an enabling learning environment that creates learning for all

PowerPoint: 30min session 4_Creating an enabling learning environment that creates learning for all

Focus	Timings	Format	Content
Introduction	7 minutes	**Presentation**	This session is focused on thinking about how you can develop an enabling environment in terms of the physical environment and how you relate to children. • Present Slides 1–5. • Each slide has a few points to reflect on.

Activity 1	7 minutes discussion
	
	 3 minutes feedback
		Group discussion	Ask attendees to get into groups of 2–3.
			 • Display Slide 6:
			   - *In terms of the physical environment of the classroom what do you do currently to transmit the message to **all** children that learning is important, learning is for everyone and that you are part of this learning environment? (Consider displays, resources, furnishings, etc.)*
			   - *How could you do this better?*
			 • For this activity also consider children with SEND and your Pupil Premium children, EAL children, looked after children and others at risk of underachievement.

		Whole-group feedback	Feed back as a group.
Activity 2	7 minutes discussion 3 minutes feedback	**Individual or group discussion**	Work through Slides 7–11. • It is suggested that this session is carried out as a discussion session. • The attendees consider the sets of questions in Slides 7–11 and can answer them individually and feed back, or as a group or a number of small groups. • The idea is to challenge current practice and consider possible ways of 'doing it better'.
Conclusion and takeaway	3 minutes	**Questions and summary**	Spend the last 3 minutes answering questions.

Session 5: Wider outcomes and opportunities

PowerPoint: 30min session 5_Wider outcomes and opportunities

Focus	Timings	Format	Content

Introduction	3 minutes	Presentation	Introduce the topic of wider outcomes and opportunities.
			• Present Slides 1–4:
			  - Activities outside the classroom.
			  - Addressing wider provision.
			  - Developing wider opportunities.

Activity 1	7 minutes discussion
	
	3 minutes feedback
		Group discussion	Ask attendees to work in groups of 2–3 and display Slide 5.
			• Reflection: wider activities
			  - *Consider the wider activities/clubs you provide – could you provide more? How do you know which ones to provide?*
			  - *Which pupils attend your extra-curricular activities?*
			  - *How could you involve more pupils in extra-curricular activities?*
			  - *Which pupils would benefit from extra-curricular activities who do not currently attend?*

		Whole-group feedback	Feed back as a group.
Presentation	3 minutes presentation 5 minutes whole-group discussion	Presentation	Present Slides 6–12. • Slide 12 should give the attendees the opportunity to put forward any thoughts they might have for developing local contacts/partnerships (e.g. governors of schools, schools their children may attend, any independent schools with which you can develop partnership, any local businesses they know, etc – and how will you approach them/ what do you want them to do?).
		Whole-group discussion	• Spend 5 minutes as a whole group contributing their thoughts. • Record the answers on the flipchart.

Focus	Timings	Format	Content
Activity 2	5 minutes discussion 3 minutes feedback	Group discussion	Ask attendees to work in their groups again and display Slide 13. • It focuses on changing cultures to develop a culture open to extra-curricular activities – and developing extra-curricular activities. *How would you respond to the following challenges through extra-curricular provision?* - *Poor attendance amongst Pupil Premium pupils.* - *Poor behaviour for learning.* - *Poor 'relationships' across the school (teacher–pupil; pupil–pupil; parent–teacher; teacher–TAs, etc.).* Feed back as a group.
Conclusion and takeaway	1 minute	Questions and summary	Spend the last 1 minute answering questions.

Sessions 6–10: Case studies

The following five sessions are based on a case study format (they are the same case studies from Part 1 so you should be familiar with the contents). Each training session follows the same structure but focuses on a different topic. Use the following table to plan each session.

- Session 6: Case study 1 – Parent and carer engagement
  PowerPoint: 30min session 6_Case study 1- parent and carer engagement

- Session 7: Case study 2 – Tracking progress in maths
  PowerPoint: 30min session 7_Case study 2- Tracking progess in maths

- Session 8: Case study 3 – SEND, differentiation and interventions
  PowerPoint: 30min session 8_Case study 3- SEND, differentiation and interventions

- Session 9: Case study 4 – Quality first teaching
  PowerPoint: 30min session 9_Case study 4- Quality first teaching

- Session 10: Case study 5 – Maths using the mastery approach
  PowerPoint: 30min session 10_Case study 5- maths using the mastery approach

Focus	Timings	Format	Content
Introduction	10 minutes	Presentation	Introduce the topic. • Present each stage of the case study; give attendees time to think and reflect on what has been done in practice.
Activity 1	10 minutes discussion 7 minutes feedback	Group discussion	Ask attendees to work in groups of 2–3 and discuss: • What strategies did the schools use? • What were the outcomes? • Which of these strategies could they use in their own classrooms?
		Whole-group discussion	Feed back as a whole group.
Conclusion and takeaway	3 minutes	Questions and summary	Answer any final questions and tell attendees to choose one idea that they will take away and put into practice in their classroom.

15-minute sessions

Planning document

Focus	Notes
Facilitators and audience	This series of 15-minute sessions is for school leaders, teachers and teaching assistants. You can get help running the sessions from the professional development co-ordinator or a key teacher/leader.
Topics covered	1. A structured approach to engaging parents and carers 2. How to review whether your assessment is effective 3. Staff with good levels of SEND knowledge 4. How to talk to children about what they know 5. How to involve children in planning 6. Four differentiation techniques you should be using 7. Targets for you 8. Action planning
Preparation tasks	• Email round the above list to staff. • The reflection questions at the end of Chapter 5, Part 1 are a useful starting point for all CPD as they enable teaching staff/school leaders and teaching assistants to reflect on their own practice before they come to the session. • Provide photocopies of the relevant reflection questions from Chapter 5, Part 1 before the session for staff to reflect on.
Resources required	You will need • PowerPoint slides • flipchart and pens • A4 paper and pens for attendees. You can send round the PowerPoint after each session.
Preparation time	• It is suggested that that you go through each PowerPoint before the session. • Familiarise yourself with it and use this book to add any extra details you want. Everyone has their own way of preparing and you must spend the time you feel you need. • This may take between 30 and 60 minutes. • 15 minutes to set up the room on the day and gather resources. • Printing is not needed.
Potential problems and solutions	Staff may feel they already do a lot to raise attainment through the various areas covered by the individual session titles. They may do, but when you focus on your practice you realise there is always more to do; there are gaps. And what we thought was great practice can overlook taking practice to the next level. The idea is to keep getting better – going from good to great. If time is taken to prepare the session and consideration given to the reflections/activities, there should be no problems in delivery and enabling staff to consider culture, change and staff leading change.

Focus	Notes
Possible follow-up tasks	The reflection activities that are done during the session are designed so that participants can 'take that away' and reflect on it further. These sessions are focused on developing individual practice in the context of whole-school improvement. It is suggested that the CPD should be accompanied by short lesson observations (peer). Staff should re-visit the reflection questions at the end of Chapter 5, Part 1 and complete the relevant section in the week following the individual session.
Pass it on	There are a number of options for 'passing it on'. • Staff giving feedback in a meeting about some aspect of their practice they changed as a result of the sessions and how that raised the attainment of pupils (or certain pupils). • Staff can implement meetings to discuss progress of pupils (data-led meetings). • Staff can develop a research group to develop practice through their own research or develop evidence-based practice.

Session step-by-step instructions

Session 1: A structured approach to engaging parents and carers

PowerPoint: 15min session 1_A structured approach to engaging parents and carers

Focus	Timings	Format	Content
Introduction	1 minute	Presentation	Introduce the structured conversation between parents or carers, the child and the child's teacher. • Use Slides 1–2.
Activity 1	5 minutes discussion 2 minutes feedback	Group discussion	Ask attendees to work in groups of 2–3 and display Slide 3. • In their groups, attendees read through how to develop the structured conversation in practice as detailed on Slide 3. • Ask the groups to discuss what teachers would want to discuss with parents regarding a way to improve teaching and learning around the child.
		Whole-group feedback	Feed back as a whole group.
Activity 2	5 minutes discussion 2 minutes feedback	Individual reflection	Now ask attendees to work individually. Display Slide 4. • Ask them to reflect on the 4 foundational blocks for effective parent and carer engagement. • What would they do to ensure the structured conversation went well? • Write at least 1 idea for each stage.
		Whole-group feedback	Feed back as a group.

Session 2: How to review whether your assessment is effective

PowerPoint: 15min session 2_How to review whether your assessment is effective

Focus	Timings	Format	Content
Introduction	1 minute	Presentation	Use Slides 1–2 to introduce what is meant by effective assessment.
Presentation	2 minutes	Presentation	Present Slide 3. • Slide 3 is the outline of a framework to help attendees consider whether their assessment is effective. • Is it showing where children are in their learning, where they are going and how they will get there?
Activity 1	10 minutes discussion 2 minutes feedback	Group discussion	Now ask attendees to work in groups of 2–3 and display Slide 4. • Ask them to reflect on their own assessment practices. • How they can make it better? • They should focus their discussion on their current strengths and gaps based on the framework in Slide 3.
		Whole-group feedback	Feed back as a group.

Session 3: Staff with good levels of SEND knowledge

PowerPoint: 15min session 3_Staff with good levels of SEND knowledge

Focus	Timings	Format	Content
Introduction	1 minute	Presentation	Use Slides 1–2 to remind staff of the areas of need set out in the Code of Practice.

Presentation	5 minutes	Presentation	Present Slides 3–6 and Slide 7.
			• These slides look more closely at some of the common needs children present with in school and the types of symptoms.
			• Emphasise that they are important for staff to know so that they can 'pick up' a SEND or potential SEND in the classroom.
			• Common needs covered in the PowerPoints are:
			  - autistic spectrum disorder
			  - Asperger's syndrome
			  - dyslexia
			  - hearing or visual impairment.
			• Slide 7 reminds staff again about the importance of involving the parents or carers and the child – giving them the opportunity to put their views across.

Activity 1	7 minutes discussion 2 minutes feedback	Group discussion	Now ask attendees to work in groups of 2–3 and display Slide 8. • Ask them to have a discussion about the most effective provision in school and that which gets the best outcomes for children. • The idea is to to start thinking about gaps and how they could be further developed.
		Whole-group feedback	Feed back as a group.

Session 4: How to talk to children about what they know

PowerPoint: 15min session 4_How to talk to children about what they know

Focus	Timings	Format	Content
Introduction	5 minutes	Presentation	Use Slides 1–5 to introduce how you can talk to children to develop their learning, including pointers towards the 'right sort' of questions.
Activity 1	8 minutes discussion 2 minutes feedback	Group discussion	Now ask attendees to work in groups of 2–3 and display Slide 6. • Get attendees to discuss how they can help children to understand the learning process. - How can they ask children questions to help them become independent learners (rather than giving them the answer)?
		Whole-group feedback	Feed back as a group.

Session 5: How to involve children in planning

PowerPoint: 15min session 5_How to involve children in planning

Focus	Timings	Format	Content
Introduction	8 minutes	Presentation	Use Slides 1–5 to introduce how to enable children to take ownership for their learning and the extent to which teachers currently address this in the classroom. • For this session, it is worth spending more time on the slides and less time on the reflection.
Activity 1	5 minutes discussion 2 minutes feedback	Group discussion	Now ask attendees to work in groups of 2–3 and display Slide 6. • Ask them to discuss and come up with ideas for how they could better involve children in planning learning.
		Whole-group feedback	Feed back as a group.

Session 6: Four differentiation techniques you should be using

PowerPoint: 15min session 6_Four differentiation techniques you should be using

Focus	Timings	Format	Content
Introduction	6 minutes	Presentation	Introduce the topic using Slides 1–2. • Define differentiation. • Next, present Slides 3–4, including the 4 differentiation techniques. Think about examples of how each of the 4 techniques is used in practice.
Activity 1	6 minutes discussion 3 minutes feedback	Group discussion	Now ask attendees to work in groups of 2–3 and display Slide 5. • Ask attendees to discuss: - What differentiation means to them.
		Whole-group feedback	- How they currently differentiate. - How they could improve their practice.

Session 7: Targets for you

PowerPoint: 15min session 7_Targets for you

Focus	Timings	Format	Content
Introduction	5 minutes	Presentation	The idea of this session is to give attendees an opportunity to focus on their own professional development in the midst of a strong focus on practices to raise attainment in the primary classroom. • Tell attendees that this session provides them with the space and the time to do this. • They may have already been thinking about it over the last few sessions. • Present Slides 1–3. • Spend about 2 minutes on Slide 4, discussing what each part of SMARTIES means in practice. • Then present Slide 5.

Activity 1	8 minutes discussion
	
	2 minutes feedback
		Individual reflection	Ask attendees to work individually and display Slide 6.
			
			• Ask them to reflect on areas of their practice they would like to improve on.
			• Then they need to set themselves 4 targets, one covering each of the following 4 areas:
			  - raising standards
			  - classroom management strategies
			  - school performance
			  - career and professional development.

		Whole-group feedback	Allow 2 minutes at the end for comment or if anyone wants to read out a target for discussion.

Session 8: Action planning

PowerPoint: 15min session 8_Action planning

Focus	Timings	Format	Content
Introduction	5 minutes	Presentation	The idea of this session is to ask staff to develop an action plan for achieving the targets they set in the previous session. • It should be noted that the process outlined in this session can be used for developing any action plan for change. • Present Slides 1–3, which consider what action planning is all about. • Then move onto Slide 4, which considers the types of questions that need to be considered to develop an effective action plan. • Slide 5 looks at further questions for action planning if a more detailed strategy is required.
Activity 1	8 minutes discussion 2 minutes feedback	Individual reflection	When you have presented all the slides, go back to Slide 4. • Ask attendees to work individually. • Ask attendees to consider the 4 targets that they set at the last session. • Ask them to develop an action plan for achieving each one.
		Whole-group feedback	Allow 2 minutes at the end for comment or if anyone wants to read out part of their action plan.

3 Evaluating the success of your CPD

To enhance the personal and professional lives of teachers, professional development needs to be clear and useful. The focus of CPD is dual, in that it should benefit the individual and at the same time it should benefit the school. More specifically, professional development should have a positive impact on learners. The following checklists provide a holistic framework for you to evaluate the success of your CPD.

Checklist: factors that can affect the impact of CPD

Focus of CPD:

- Relevance to staff.
- Relevance to the school improvement plan.
- Relevance to improving teaching and learning.
- The degree of leverage.

Context of CPD:

- Synergy in relation to other policies or initiatives.
- Values, aspirations and interests of those who develop it.
- The structure and quality of leadership in the school.
- The structure and quality of external frameworks of support and challenge.
- Organisational structures and processes within the school.
- The culture within the school.

Process of CPD:

- The quality and appropriateness of information and evidence on which proposals for change are based.
- The effectiveness and dissemination of information and evidence.
- The extent and intensity of the participation of relevant members of the school community.
- The quality and appropriateness of strategic action plans.
- The effectiveness of leadership and support.
- The effectiveness of co-ordination between development activities.
- The effectiveness of monitoring and evaluation of work in progress.

Checklist: impact on staff

Classroom practice:

- Use of new practices by staff.
- Use of new practices by teacher's colleagues.

- Improvement of the effectiveness of established practices on the part of staff.
- Improvement of the effectiveness of established practices on the part of colleagues.

Personal capacity:

- Increase in pedagogical knowledge and skills.
- Increase in professional knowledge.
- Development of new strategies for professional learning (e.g. engaging with research).
- Development of personal attributes (e.g. more reflective on practice, more self-confident in practice and trying out new practices).
- Enhanced clarity of purpose and commitment.

Interpersonal capacity:

- Enhanced level of participation or involvement.
- Development of skills in building and maintaining professional relationships.

Checklist: impact on the school as an organisation

Structures and processes:

- More effective structures for reflection and decision-making.
- Improvement in the structure of leadership.
- Greater degree of distributed/shared leadership.
- More collaborative working patterns.

Culture and capacity:

- Increase in the use of evidence.
- Improved collegial relationships.
- Improvements in the quality of professional discussion.
- Higher level of consistency in practice.
- Greater levels of agreement in beliefs and values.

Checklist: impact beyond the school

- Contributions to debate with the research community.
- Contributions to policy formation or critique of policies.
- Dissemination of evidence-based practice.

- Collaborative development work with other staff and schools.
- Improved levels of social capital in the local community.

Checklist: impact on pupils' learning

Attainment:

- Improved attainment.
- Improved rate of progress.
- Learning in other curriculum areas (e.g. citizenship).
- Discernible increases in subject knowledge, understanding and skills.
- Improvement in transferable and key skills.

Dispositions:

- Development of more positive attitudes to school.
- Increased motivation to learn.
- Increased confidence and self-esteem.
- Improvement in the quality of relationships.

Metacognition:

- Development of self-awareness.
- Increased capacity to reflect on and evaluate their own learning.
- More able to take responsibility for their own learning.

Checklist: evidence of impact

It is important to collect evidence on the impact of professional development. The following checklist will help you to do that.

The gathering and use of evidence plays a key role in maximising impact.

- Evidence generated for other professional purposes is analysed to determine impact (assessment of pupils' work).
- Monitoring and evaluation is part of the framework of support and challenge for development work provided by senior staff or external agents.
- Evidence is gathered deliberately and systematically to inform and sharpen development work.
- The gathering of evidence of impact and collaborative reflection on it helps to build organisational capacity.

Identifying SMART targets

The next stage for teachers/managers and teams is to work together on identifying SMART targets for action. The following can be developed as a workshop to help focus individual and collective targets.

Establishing agreement on good practice

Purpose:
To establish agreed perceptions/indicators of good practice in teaching/learning through building a common list of questions/statements.

Materials:
A flipchart

Time:
1 hour

- Decide on the goal for the particular professional development activity.
- Specify the objectives, which are SMART (*Specific, Measurable, Attainable, Relevant and Timely*).
- List questions for: monitoring, evaluation and review.
- Devise a time-reporting plan for completion of monitoring, evaluation and review of professional development activities.

Conclusion

As professionals, staff view the school in which they work as a place of learning and development. For all members of the school community, learning and development are central to the process of schooling. Whilst it is axiomatic that schools provide learning and development opportunities for pupils, schools should also provide a learning environment for all staff – teaching and non-teaching. The expertise and experience of teachers and support staff are a school's most valuable resources. Your personal and professional development will give you a stronger role in the achievement of all children and better enable you to push back against any practice that does not improve their life chances through education.

Bibliography

Achievement for All (2018) 'Every child included in education manifesto', Newbury: Achievement for All. Available at: https://afaeducation.org/media/1489/afa-manifesto-final-2205.pdf

Alexander, R. (ed.) (2009) *Children, Their World, Their Education: Final Report and Recommendations of the Cambridge Primary Review*, Abingdon: Routledge.

AQR International (2017) 'Understanding "soft skills" development at independent schools: an analysis of mental toughness at UK independent schools'.

Assessment Reform Group (ARG) (2002) *Assessment for Learning: 10 Principles*, ARG.

Bennett, T. (2017) 'Creating a culture: how school leaders can optimise behaviour', London: Department for Education. Crown copyright. Available at: https://assets.publishing.service.gov.uk/government/uploads/system/uploads/attachment_data/file/602487/Tom_Bennett_Independent_Review_of_Behaviour_in_Schools.pdf

Black, P. and Wiliam, D. (1998) *Inside the Black Box: Raising Standards Through Classroom Assessment*, London: GL Assessment.

Blandford, S. (2004) *Professional Development Manual: A Practical Guide to Planning and Evaluating Successful Staff Development* (3rd edn.), Harlow: Pearson Education.

Blandford, S. (2006) *Middle Leadership in Schools: Harmonising Leadership and Learning*, Harlow: Pearson/Longman.

Blandford, S. (2015) *Don't Like Mondays?*, Woodbridge: John Catt.

Blandford, S. (2015) 'Great teaching – is it enough?' *Education Today*, 65, (2), 24–8.

Blandford, S. (2015) *Love to Teach: Bring Out the Best in You and Your Class*, Woodbridge: John Catt.

Blandford, S. (2015) *Make School Better*, Woodbridge: John Catt.

Blandford, S. (2015) *Take The Lead*, Woodbridge: John Catt.

Blandford, S. (2017) *Born to Fail? Social Mobility: A Working Class View*, Woodbridge: John Catt.

Blandford, S. and Knowles, C. (2013) *Achievement for All: Raising Aspirations, Access and Achievement*, London: Bloomsbury.

Blandford, S. and Knowles, C. (2016) *Developing Professional Practice 0–7* (2nd edn.), Abingdon: Routledge.

Blandford, S., Travlos, L., Williams, K., Crowhurst, M. and Knowles, C. (2011) *Achievement for All Anthology*, Newbury: Achievement for All.

Bogdan, R. and Biklin, S. K. (2017) *Qualitative Research for Education: An Introduction to Theories and Methods* (5th edn.), Boston, MA: Pearson.

Bolam, R. (1993) 'Recent developments and emerging issues in the continuing professional development of teachers', London: General Teaching Council of England and Wales.

Booth, T. and Ainscow, M. (2011) *Index for Inclusion: Developing Learning and Participation in Schools*, Bristol: CSIE.

Clarke, S. (1998) *Targeting Assessment in the Primary Classroom*, Abingdon, Oxon: Hodder and Stoughton.

Clarke, S. (2002) *Formative Assessment in Action: Weaving the Elements Together*, Abingdon, Oxon: Hodder Murray.

Coe, R., Aloisi, C., Higgins, S. and Elliot Major, L. (2014) 'What makes great teaching? Review of the underpinning research', London: Sutton Trust. Available at: https://www.suttontrust.com/wp-content/uploads/2014/10/What-Makes-Great-Teaching-REPORT.pdf

Cohen, L., Manion, L. and Morrison, K. (2017) *Research Methods in Education* (8th edn.), Abingdon: Routledge.

Coleman, M. and Bush, T. (1994) 'Managing with teams', in T. Bush and J. West-Burnham (eds.), *The Principles of Educational Management*, Harlow: Longman.

Collins, K. (2018) 'First early years setting joins growing network of 23 Research Schools', EEF News. Available at: https://educationendowmentfoundation.org.uk/pdf/generate/?u=https://educationendowmentfoundation.org.uk/pdf/

content/?id=2424&e=2424&t=First%2oearly%2oyears%2osetting%2ojoins%2o
growing%2onetwork%2oof%2023%2oResearch%2oSchools&s=&mode=embed

Cordingley, P. (2013) 'The contribution of research to teachers' professional
learning and development'. Available at: https://www.bera.ac.uk/
wp-content/uploads/2013/12/BERA-Paper-5-Continuing-professional-development-
and-learning.pdf

Crown (2015) 'Final report of the commission on assessment without levels',
London: Crown.

Cullinane, C. and Montacute, R. (2017) 'Life lessons: improving essential life skills
for young people', London: Sutton Trust.

Department for Education (2014) 'Assessment principles', London: DfE. Crown
copyright. Available at: http://www.bsp.london/wp-content/uploads/2015/01/
Assessment_Principles-from-DfE-2015.pdf

Department for Education/Department of Health (2013) 'SEND pathfinder
information packs, 0–25 coordinated assessment process and education, health
and care (EHC) plan', London: DfE/DoH.

Department for Education/Department of Health (2015) 'SEND 0–25 Code of
Practice', London: DfE/DoH.

Dunford, J. (2014) 'Ten point plan for spending the pupil premium successfully'.
Available at: https://johndunfordconsulting.co.uk/2014/10/11/ten-point-
plan-for-spending-the-pupil-premium-successfully/

Dweck, C. (2000) *Self-Theories: Their Role in Motivation, Personality and Development*,
Hove: Psychology Press.

Epstein, M., Atkins, M., Cullinan, D., Kutash, K., and Weaver, R. (2008) *Reducing
Behavior Problems in the Elementary School Classroom: A Practice Guide* (NCEE
#2008–012). Washington, DC: National Center for Education Evaluation and Regional
Assistance, Institute of Education Sciences, U.S. Department of Education.

Everard, K. B. (1986) *Developing Management in Schools*, Oxford: Blackwell.

Everard, K. B., Morris, G. and Wilson, I. (2004) *Effective School Management* (4th
edn.), London: Paul Chapman Publishing.

Evertson, C. M. and Weinstein, C. S. (2013) *Handbook of Classroom Management:
Research, Practice, and Contemporary Issues*, Abingdon: Routledge.

Fidler, B. (2002) *Strategic Management for School Development*, London: Paul Chapman.

Goldacre, B. (2013) 'Building evidence into education', London: Department for Education.

Goodall, J., Vorhaus, J., Carpentieri, J., Brooks, G., Akerman, R. and Harris, A. (2011) 'Review of best practice in parental engagement', Nottingham: DfE.

Gorard, S., Huat See, B. and Davies, P. (2012) *The Impact of Attitudes and Aspirations on Educational Attainment and Participation*, York: Joseph Rowntree Foundation.

Hackman, R. and Walton, R. (1986) 'Heading groups in organisations', in Goodman, P. (ed.), *Designing Effective Workshops*, San Francisco, CA: Jossey-Bass.

Hall, V. and Oldroyd, D. (1990) *Management Self-development for Staff in Secondary Schools, Unit 1: Self-development for Effective Management*, Bristol: NDCEMP.

Handscomb, G. and MacBeath, J. (2003) 'The Research Engaged School', Chelmsford, Forum for Learning and Research Enquiry (FLARE), Essex County Council.

Handy, C. (1993) *Understanding Schools as Organizations* (4th edn.), Harmondsworth: Penguin.

Handy, C. and Aitkin, R. (1986) *Understanding Schools as Organizations*, Hamondsworth: Penguin.

Hargreaves, D. H. (1995) 'Self-managing schools and development planning - chaos or control?' *School Organisation*, 15, (3), 215–17.

Hargreaves, D. H. and Hopkins, D. (1991) 'School effectiveness, school improvement and development planning', in Preedy, M. (ed.), *Managing the Effective School*, London: Paul Chapman Publishing.

Harris, A. (2013) *Distributed Leadership Matters: Perspectives, Practicalities, and Potential*, London: Sage.

Harris, A. and Goodall, J. (2007) 'Engaging parents in raising achievement. Do parents know they matter?' Department for Children, Schools and Families.

Harrison, H. and Howard, S. (2009) *Inside the Primary Black Box*, London: GL Assessment.

Hart, A. and Green, S. (2014) 'Fostering academic resilience: a brief review of the evidence', University of Brighton and Boingboing Social Enterprise for YoungMinds. (Available as a PDF document online.)

Henry, C. (2013) 'The inspection of provision for learners who have learning difficulties and/or disabilities', London: Ofsted (Action for Inclusion Conference, November 2013).

Humphrey, N. and Squires, G. (2011) 'Achievement for All, National Evaluation: Final Report'. Nottingham: Department for Education.

Impetus (2014) *Make NEETs History*, London: Impetus.

Jones, P. (2008) *Tycoon*, London: Hodder and Stoughton.

Jones, C., and Pound, L. (2008) *Leadership and Management in the Early Years: A Practical Guide*, Maidenhead: Open University Press.

Judkins, M., Stacey, O., McCrone, T. and Inniss, M. (2014) 'Teachers' use of research evidence: a case study of United Learning schools', Slough: NFER.

Kemmis, S. and Carr, W. (1986) *Becoming Critical: Education Knowledge and Action Research*, Abingdon: Deakin University Press.

Knowles, C. (2017) 'Closing the attainment gap in maths: a study of good practice in early years and primary settings', London: Fair Education Alliance. Available at: https://static1.squarespace.com/static/543e665de4b0fbb2b140b291/t/58aaeac4296 87f223f0ff369/1487596235907/FEA+Numeracy+Report_FV.pdf

Larson, C. E. and LaFasto F. M. J. (1989) *Teamwork: What Must Go Right, What Can Go Wrong*, Newbury Park, CA: Sage.

Lewin, K. (1946) 'Action research and minority problems', in G. W. Lewin (ed.) *Resolving Social Conflicts*. New York, NY: Harper & Row.

Lincoln, J. (1982) 'Intra- (and inter-) organisational networks', *Research in the Sociology of Organisations*, 1, (1), 1–18.

Macleod, S., Sharp, C., Bernardinelli, D., Skipp, A. and Higgins S. (2015) 'Supporting the attainment of disadvantaged pupils: articulating success and good practice', research report, November, London: Department for Education.

Manchester LEA (1986), *Model for Self-Evaluation*, Manchester: Manchester LEA.

Marshall, P. (2013) *The Tail: How England's Schools Fail One Child in Five – and What Can be Done*, London: Profile Books Ltd.

Maslow, A. H. (1943) 'A theory of human motivation', *Psychological Review*, 50,(4), 370–396.

Maughan, S., Teeman, D., and Wilson, R. (2012) *What Leads to Positive Change in Teaching Practice*, NFER Research Programme: Developing the Education Workforce.

Mayo, E. (1933) *The Human Problems of an Individual Civilisation*, London: MacMillan.

Millburn, A. (2009) 'Unleashing aspiration: the final report of the panel on fair access to the professions', London: The Panel on Fair Access to the Professions. Crown copyright.

NAHT (2014) *Report of the NAHT Commission on Assessment*, London: NAHT.

NfER (2007) 'Getting to grips with assessment: primary. Starting out in assessment'. Available at: www.nfer.ac.uk/pdf/getting-to-grips-with-assessment-1.pdf

Northouse, P. (2004) *Leadership: Theory and Practice*, Thousand Oaks, California: Sage Publications.

Nuffield Foundation, www.nuffieldfoundation.org/assessment-reform-group

OECD (2012), 'Equity and quality in education: supporting disadvantaged students and schools', Paris: OECD.

OECD (2016), 'Low-performing students: why they fall behind and how to help them succeed', UK Country Note, Paris: OECD.

Ofsted (2008) 'Learning outside the classroom', London: Ofsted. Crown copyright.

Ofsted (2013) 'The Pupil Premium: how schools are spending the funding successfully to maximise achievement', London: Ofsted. Crown copyright.

Ormston, M. and Shaw, M. (1993) *Mentoring*, Oxford Brookes University, School of Education.

Overall, L. and Sangster, M. (2006) *Assessment: A Practical Guide for Primary Teachers*, London: Bloomsbury.

Parsons, D. and Burkey, S. (2011) *Evaluation of the Teaching and Learning Research Programme (Second Phase)*. London: ESRC.

Poulson, L. and Wallace, M. (2004) *Learning to Read Critically in Teaching and Learning*, London: Sage.

Preedy, M. (1991) *Managing the Effective School*, London: Paul Chapman.

Pugh, D. and Hickson, D. (1989) *Writers on Organisations* (4th edn.), Harmondsworth: Penguin.

PwC (2015) 'Interim achieving schools, social impact assessment report', Belfast: PwC.

PwC (2016) '2011–2016 achieving schools, social impact assessment report', Belfast: PwC.

Sammons, P., Toth, K. and Sylva, K. (2015) 'Subject to background: what promotes better achievement of bright but disadvantaged students?' London: Sutton Trust.

Schleicher, A. (2014) 'Equity, excellence and inclusiveness in education: policy lessons from around the world', Paris: OECD.

Senge, P. M. (1990) *The Fifth Discipline - The Art and Practice of the Learning Organization*, New York: Double Day.

Sharples, J., Slavin, R., Chambers, B. and Sharp, C. (2011) *Effective Classroom Strategies for Closing the Gap in Educational Achievement for Children and Young People Living in Poverty, Including White Working-Class Boys* (C4EO Schools and Communities Research Review 4), London: C4EO

Shaw, B., Bernardes, E., Trethewey, A. and Menzies, L. (2016) *Special Educational Needs and Their Links to Poverty*, York: Joseph Rowntree Foundation.

Shepard, L. A., Hammerness, K., Darling-Hammond, L., Rust, F., Snowden, J. B., Gordon, E., Gutierrez, C. and Pacheco, A. (2005) 'Assessment', in L. Darling-Hammond and J. Bransford (eds.), *Preparing Teachers for a Changing World: What Teachers Should Learn and be Able to Do*, San Francisco, CA: Jossey-Bass, pp. 275–326.

Simonsen, B., Fairbanks, S., Briesch, A., Myers, D. and Sugai, G. (2008) 'Evidence-based practices in classroom management: considerations for research to practice', *Education and Treatment of Children*, 31, (3), 351–80.

Social Mobility and Child Poverty Commission (2015), 'State of the nation 2015: social mobility and child poverty', London: Social Mobility and Child Poverty Commission.

Steer, A. (2009) 'Learning behaviour: the report of the practitioners group on school behaviour and discipline', Nottingham: Department for Education and Skills. Crown copyright.

Stephenson, C. (2005) 'The essence of great leadership', *Ivey Business Journal* January/February 2005.

Sutton Trust (2011) 'Improving the impact of teachers on pupil achievement in the UK – interim findings', London: Sutton Trust.

Sutton Trust (2015) 'The Social Mobility Index', London: Sutton Trust.

Sutton Trust and Education Endowment Foundation (2015) 'The Pupil Premium: Next Steps', London: Sutton Trust.

Taylor, F. W. (1947) *Scientific Management*, London: Harper and Row.

Tomlinson, C. (1999) *The Differentiated Classroom: Responding to the needs of all learners*, Virginia: ASCD.

Tomlinson, C. and Parrish, W. (2013) 'Defensible differentiation: why, what, and how?' Available at: http://www.caroltomlinson.com/Presentations/Tomlinson%20 ASL%20Institute%206-13%20V2.pdf

Treadaway, M. (2017) 'Long-term disadvantage, part one: challenges and successes', London: Education Datalab. Available at: https://ffteducationdatalab.org. uk/2017/07/long-term-disadvantage-part-one-challenges-and-successes/

Truss, E. (2014) 'The Spectator's schools conference on delivering world class schools', London, 1st April.

Tuckman, B. W. (1965) 'Development sequence in small groups', *Psychological Bulletin*, 63, (6), 384–99.

West, N. (1995) *Middle Management in the Primary School*, London: David Fulton.

Wheater, R., Durbib, B., McNamara, S. and Classick, R. (2016) 'Is mathematics education in England working for everyone? NfER analysis of the PISA performance of disadvantaged pupils', Slough: NfER.

Whitebread, D., Anderson, H., Coltman, P., Page, C., Pino Pasternak, D. and Mehta, S. (2005) 'Developing independent learning in the early years', *Education 3–13*, March.

Williams, J. (2003) *Promoting Independent Learning in the Primary Classroom*, Buckingham: Open University Press.

Williams, J. (2015) 'Free to pursue an academic education', in A. de Waal (ed.), *The Ins and Outs of Selective Secondary Schools*, Civitas: London.

Yeo, A. and Graham, J. (2015) 'A deep dive into social and emotional learning: what do the views of those involved tell us about the challenges for policy-makers?' EIF/ Cabinet Office/Social Mobility and Child Poverty Commission/ReachAbility.

Index